The Early Years of Folk Music

Fifty Founders of the Tradition

DAVID DICAIRE

McFarland & Company, Inc., Publishers
Jefferson, North Carolina, and London

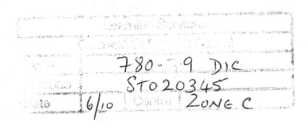
LIBRARY OF CONGRESS CATALOGUING-IN-PUBLICATION DATA

Dicaire, David, 1963–
    The early years of folk music : fifty founders of the tradition /
David Dicaire.
        p.   cm.
    Includes bibliographical references and index.

    ISBN 978-0-7864-4431-1
    softcover : 50# alkaline paper

    1. Folk music — History and criticism.
    2. Folk musicians — Biography.   I. Title.
    ML3545.D56   2010
    781.620092' 2 — dc22   2010002491
    [B]

British Library cataloguing data are available

On the cover: Woody Guthrie 1930s; Josh White; Pete Seeger,
1947; guitar ©2009 Shutterstock

Manufactured in the United States of America

McFarland & Company, Inc., Publishers
    Box 611, Jefferson, North Carolina 28640
    www.mcfarlandpub.com

The Early Years
of Folk Music

To the common folk around the world
who continue to struggle

Contents

Introduction 1

Part One. Historical Figures 7
Thomas D'Urfey (1653–1723), English Folk Comic 9
Turlough O'Carolan (1670–1738), The Gaelic Harpist 12
Denis O'Hampsey (1695–1807), Harp Magic 15
Niel Gow (1727–1807), Scottish Fiddle Dance Master 19
Edward Bunting (1773–1843), The Transcriber 22
Targjei Augundsson (1801–1872), Father of Norwegian Folk 25
Ostap Veresai (1803–1899), Ukrainian Minstrel 28
Francis J. Child (1825–1896), The Collector 31
Cecil Sharp (1859–1924), Folklore Revivalist 33

Part Two. American Pioneers 37
Stephen Foster (1826–1864), Father of American Folk Music 39
John A. Lomax (1867–1948), The Ballad Hunter 44
Bascom Lamar Lunsford (1882–1973), Minstrel of the
  Appalachians 48
Charles Seeger (1886–1979), American Musicologist 52
Aunt Molly Jackson (1880–1960), Pistol Packing Mama 55
Helen Flanders (1890–1972), The Vermont Songcatcher 59
John Jacob Niles (1892–1980), Dean of American Balladeers 64
Elizabeth Cotten (1893–1987), The Fingerpicker 67
Clarence Ashley (1895–1967), The Blue Ridge Entertainer 71
Dock Boggs (1898–1971), Primeval Hillbilly Folk 75

Buell Kazee (1900–1976), Lonesome Balladeer 78

Ruth Crawford Seeger (1901–1953), Folk Music Matriarch 81

Part Three. Political Connections 85

Joe Hill (1879–1915), The Initiator 87

Burl Ives (1909–1995), The Wayfarin' Stranger 90

Earl Robinson (1910–1991), Ballad for Americans 96

Woody Guthrie (1912–1967), Bound for Glory 99

Lee Hays (1914–1981), Lonesome Traveler 109

Josh White (1914–1969), Folk-Blues Protest 112

Cisco Houston (1918–1961), The Pure Voice 119

Joe Glazer (1918–2006), Labor's Troubadour 123

Pete Seeger (1919–), Twentieth Century Folk Man 126

Fred Hellerman (1927–), The Little Cowboy 133

Part Four. Folk Around the World 139

Béla Bartók (1881–1945), The Hungarian Ethnomusicologist . . . 141

Udi Hrant Kenkulian (1901–1978), The Oud Master 146

Atahualpa Yupanqui (1908–1992), Modern Argentine Folk King . 149

Luiz Gonzaga (1912–1989), Forró Folk 153

Edith Fowke (1913–1996), Canadian Folklorist 158

Vassilis Tsitsanis (1915–1984), Urban Greek Folkie 161

Amália Rodrigues (1920–1999), Voice of Portugal 165

Buddy MacMaster (1924–), Dean of Cape Breton Fiddlers 171

Hamza El Din (1929–2006), Nubian Folk Master 174

Severino Dias De Oliveira (1930–2006), Sivuca 180

Part Five. The Pre–Folk Boom Era 185

Hobart Smith (1897–1965), Blue Ridge Legacy 187

Moses Asch (1905–1986), Folkways Founder 190

A.L. Lloyd (1908–1982), Father of English Folk 194

Richard Dyer-Bennet (1913–1991), Renaissance Man 199

Alan Lomax (1915–2002), Folksong Revivalist 203

Ewan MacColl (1915–1989), English Folk Revivalist 209

Oscar Brand (1920–), The Can-Am Folklorist 215

Jean Ritchie (1922–), The Mother of Folk 220

Harry Smith (1923–1991), The Anthologist 224

Bibliography 229

Index 233

Introduction

Folk music — more than any style — has always been the voice of the common people. From the beginning of civilization throughout the construction of modern, urban centers in every corner of the globe, the genre has always managed to find a supportive group. Each regional culture can boast of a unique strain passed along (usually in an oral tradition) from one generation to another, and in many countries this practice dates back several hundred and often thousands of years. In order to truly understand the power, beauty and importance of folk music, one must first comprehend its deep, rich and diversified history.

The loosest definition of the term "folk music" dates back to the first appearance of humankind. Although debate over the true cradle of civilization rages among scholars, arguably, there was some form of simple, yet distinct vocal (chant) and instrumental sound produced in all of the ancient regions of Mesopotamia, Egypt, the Yellow River (China), and the Indus Valley (India).

The first musical instrument was the voice. Gradually, primitive instruments that reflected the economic, technical and cultural environments in which people lived and which reflected their psychological makeup were created to keep time and accompany vocal delivery. Music became a means of celebration and communication.

It also spread from the aforementioned cradles of civilization throughout other regions of the world and was shaped to suit particular needs. For example, the variety and depth of African sound reflected the diverse indigenous tribes that populated the continent, with much of this development deeply rooted in individual rhythm and tonal languages. Since the songs used no genuine lyrical system, dance was an intrinsic element in preserving the traditional sound.

In ancient Greece, music played an integral part in the daily life of the average citizen. It was present in marriages, funerals, religious ceremonies, staged dramas and the ballad-like reciting of epic poetry. The aulos, a woodwind consisting of a pair of cylindrical pipes with double reed mouthpieces,

1

and the cithara, a wooden type of lyre, were the principal instruments. In China, the guqin, a very long zither, was in use. In Persia, historical evidence points to the early notations of a diatonic scale. In Ur, part of Mesopotamia, now Iran, the bull harp was dominant. In Egypt, the lyre served as part of the court orchestra along with a type of hammered dulcimer.

A few centuries later, in Europe, popular songs were rooted in the daily life of the peasant society, integrated into work and customs. In France during the tenth century, roots music with links to the church was being created at a rapid pace. Two hundred years later, Paris boasted important entertainment centers and a strong cast of street performers. In Ireland, before the establishment of Christianity, a very basic strain of music evolved throughout the next thousand years making Ireland, in the opinion of many, the cradle of folk music.

Before and after the first millennium, folk music flourished globally. In the ancient civilizations of the Mayas, Incas and Aztecs, complex rhythms and dance rituals that celebrated death, war, marriage, peace and birth were developed, fueled by customized instruments including various drums, whistles, zithers, trumpets and flutes. In Asia, which had strong regional styles, the busy East-West trade along the silk route brought a rich mix of culture, religion and art. In India, the 5000-year-old musical tradition boasted street musicians who plied their trade in crowded markets to earn a few pennies.

The medieval period in Europe was one of suppression, and the development of music was stunted. The leading musicians on the continent were the French troubadours, jongleurs and trouvères, who, as early minstrels, meshed poetry with sound. The most celebrated was Adam de la Halle. In England, Scotland and Ireland, songs were passed down orally from one generation to another and the region usually dominated the subject matter. For example, people more closely associated with sailing, ships, and the water were apt to sing sea chanteys. In Russia, Italy, Germany, Poland, the Netherlands, Japan, China, and throughout the entire Arabic world, folk music was melodic, but also very closely related to dance.

Sadly, much of the progress made in pre–Renaissance folk music was lost due to repression. As Christianity spread through medieval Europe, the art of making folk music was associated with heathen rites and customs, and it was believed that the practice was linked to dark forces. This ideology spilled over into other inhabited continents, and because of this, the development of traditional music was stifled for many years.

During this period, the strongest strain of everyday music was in the great cathedrals, as well as the tiny churches that dominated the life of the average peasant. The meshing of religious themes with ordinary subject matter was common. The ruling noble families under the feudal system were enchanted with the art song and these reigned in their secular courts.

On a more common level, the troubadours in France and the German minnesingers were prominent throughout the continent plying their trade in the middle-class guilds that dotted every major city. It was a dangerous manner of earning a living, but the passion for making music remained in the hearts of many, including those in Ireland and Scotland, where a harp tradition was well established. The evolution of these string masters would produce some of the greatest tunes in the entire folk catalog. These lyrics and melodies would be kept alive through memory. Despite the lack of progress by the end of the middle ages, two-part songs had been developed, mainly in the court of Burgundy.

The arts flourished during the Renaissance and the folk music of each nation benefited tremendously from the renewed spark of the human spirit. The secular song enjoyed many notable changes and the polyphonic chanson was the leading style of the day. In Spain, musicians accompanied the lyrical tunes with the lute, a type of early guitar, which enhanced the old material. In the sixteenth century, the first book of lute songs was printed. The pear-shaped instrument was derived from the Arabic oud.

In Italy, where the Renaissance began, the introduction of opera would have an immeasurable impact on the art song. Different vocal forms that were prominent in musical theater pieces such as recitative and aria were integrated with folk tunes to create something fresh. The influence of this rebirth in the arts would have an incalculable effect around the globe and reverberate throughout the following centuries.

The settlement of North America extended the folk music of the Old World as the settlers brought over English, Irish and Scottish airs, which remained intact for 200 years before patriotism forced lyrical and melodic changes. Later, immigrants from other cultures created a true melting pot of sound. Music provided an escape in the lives of those who ventured to create a different life amidst the untamed wilderness.

In the colonies of New France, the voyageurs brought their chansons along to make paddling from one center to another through dangerous territory more bearable. These songs survive to this day. The East Coast with its strong Irish, Scottish and English presence would develop its own brand of Celtic folk music whose richness continues to dominate in the twenty-first century. In Quebec, les Habitants developed a unique sound that was based on their French heritage.

One of the most important folk strains in North America comes from the First Nations people. Their sound encompassed diverse, complicated, and syncopated arrangements of chants and rhythms, as well as intricate dance steps. Like many European, Asian, and South American peoples, Native Americans preserved their important creations through an oral, generational tradition which still exists to this day.

For the next 200 years, folk music remained a viable force in the culture of many countries, but was never given the attention of the classical music which dominated Europe. The great symphonies and operas were truly created for the nobility, the well-to-do, not the common people. It was in Ireland, Scotland, England and North America that the Western traditional sound was kept alive.

In the eighteenth and especially in the nineteenth century, a desire arose to preserve hundreds of years of folk material. Long before the terms musicologist or ethnomusicologist were coined, many enthusiastic individuals took it upon themselves to save the rich musical vein of English, Scottish and Irish songs. This spirited effort was echoed throughout many other countries as a sense of nationalism spurred scholars to conserve the cultural heritage for posterity. During this period, collectors emerged to play a vital role in preserving the tradition.

In the United States, folk music would take on diverse forms dictated by region. For example, in the Appalachians, many of the songs brought over from England, Scotland and Ireland served as a basis for what later became country music. The spirituals of the plantation slaves eventually provided the foundation for the blues. In New Orleans, the combination of black sacred hymns, French folk tunes, and European classical airs would form the bedrock of jazz. Because of its central location on the Mississippi trade route, the Big Easy was a crossroads of musical styles and all were assimilated into one cohesive sound. In Texas and further west, a need to project heroic stories through song would create a variant of country and western known as cowboy tunes.

America needed a writer with a frontier spirit, someone who could unite all of the regional strains into one cohesive national sound, to develop its own proper folk music identity. Stephen Foster, an Easterner with an affinity for Southern sensibilities, arrived with a banjo on his knee fresh from betting on some old nag at the Camptown races. He became the most vital American songwriter of the nineteenth century. The compositions "Camptown Races," "Oh, Susanna," "My Old Kentucky Home," "Old Black Joe," "Beautiful Dreamer," and "Old Folks at Home" ("Swannee River") became part of the nation's psyche.

There were others who made notable contributions, including Daniel Decatur Emmett and Charles K. Harris, who penned "After the Ball," an early popular hit. However, none matched Foster's expansive catalog of national treasures, which continue to be sung today throughout the country as well as the world. Despite the interruption of the Civil War, American folk music thrived with the growth of the nation.

The appeal of the homegrown popular tune spread quickly through the sale of sheet music. Many homes boasted a piano, and sing-alongs occurred in parlors across the nation, where the works of Stephen Foster and others filled the air. There were also patriotic hymns, most notably Francis Scott Key's "The Star Spangled Banner," which was declared the national anthem in 1914. At the outbreak of World War I, numbers such as "Over There" swept through North America, while the Germans popularized their own battle anthems.

Since its inception in North America, folk music had been performed for all types of celebrations, as well as around campfires, and on back porches. But with the advent of the industrial revolution and the struggle of the working class, simple, happy tunes became political anthems that enabled many to endure bloody, violent strikes. It was the first time music was used as a weapon to improve the lot of the common person, and folk music remained the voice of the people.

Another transformation in folk came about with the birth of the recording industry. The tradition of passing songs orally from one generation to the next faded with the advent of technology, as the music was made available on blues, country and jazz records. A good portion of the material in every artist's repertoire had no credited author, and many assigned their own names to reworked tunes they recorded, which earned them much-needed royalties.

Eventually, if it is to survive, every genre needs to produce a hero, someone larger than life, to personify and broadcast that particular style. The blues had Bessie Smith; country had Jimmie Rodgers; jazz had Louis Armstrong, and folk had Woody Guthrie. He emerged from the Dust Bowl region to bring the style the respect and attention it deserved. He elevated the music he loved to a much higher level than anyone before him. His dominance ensured that folk music would have an honored place in the United States and in traditional music around the world.

In the 1930s, with the country and most of the world mired in a deep economic depression, folk music played a vital role in another type of protest. A few years later, while everyone was dancing to the beat of the Big Band jazz era, folk provided gritty tunes and opened a window on the atrocities of war. But the winds of change were slowly beginning to shift.

At the beginning of the 1950s, the McCarthy hearings wreaked havoc on the folk industry, as many practitioners were prohibited from appearing at concert halls, on the radio, on television or in Hollywood. But once the "red scare" was over, the style returned with a vengeance in a back-to-the-roots campaign that spread across college campuses. The traditional sound was catapulted into the spotlight and coffeehouses opened up throughout urban centers overnight. The American revival would spur a global interest.

This book is dedicated to the contributions of the early figures of folk music, including collectors, songwriters, ethnomusicologists, musicians and singers. Despite occasional suppression and a lack of respect, today the genre is celebrated around the world in the largest cities, in rural areas, in small towns, and in the tiniest villages. Every country has its own folk music.

In an attempt to honor this ancient tradition as well as the major aspects of the style, the book has been divided into five sections. "Historical Figures" is dedicated to some of the important early figures from the seventeenth century to just before the twentieth century. "American Pioneers" honors those who forged a distinct sound in the United States. "Political Connections" explores those who fused their simple, acoustic music with a strong protest message. The fourth section celebrates those considered vital in the development of their ethnic roots in places other than England, Ireland, Scotland and the United States. The fifth part explores the years before the folk boom and those who contributed to the "golden years."

Folk is a basic style that nearly everyone has at one time or another embraced, either as a child or an adult. The lyrics and the melodies have been sung and taught to each successive generation of schoolchildren around campfires, at bedtime, in churches, at rallies, at recitals, in personal vehicles on long trips, and in many other places. Folk has been — and always will be — the music of the common people.

PART ONE

Historical Figures

Unlike blues, jazz and country, folk music stretches back hundreds, and, in some countries, thousands of years. Unfortunately, because of poor preservation and the lack of recording technology, the vital contributions of many of the important figures were lost. However, due to the efforts of a few individuals, some of this music was rescued, and the people who created it are considered the forerunners of the modern folk movement. Contributors included composers, musicians, transcribers, and, later on, collectors, who also served as historians.

The composers are the most ambiguous group. Authorship is difficult to discover for folksongs, which usually have unknown origins and are passed on, preserved and adapted, often in several different versions in an oral tradition. However, two individuals penned material indirectly related to later efforts: Thomas D'Urfey and Charles Dibdin. The former wrote satire while the latter was known for patriotic and sentimental tunes.

It wasn't until much later that people put their names on the songs they wrote in order to collect royalties. Once composers were able to benefit, the era of the singer-songwriter began. Although performers were eager to present original compositions to the listening audience, they all mixed self-penned tunes with well-known standards to keep crowds interested.

Many of the early folk figures were traveling minstrels, individuals with minor instrumental ability and adequate word skills. Their repertoire was derived from a variety of sources. It was borrowed from other musicians, self-penned, or was lyrical poetry set to music. Musical progress coincided with the evolution of more sophisticated instruments.

Each country had specific instruments which produced a unique ethnic music. For example, the lute, derived from the ud or oud, an Arabian instrument, was introduced into Europe around the tenth century and spread through the continent rather quickly. It gained an independent form some 300 years later. While there were interesting practitioners, including Mary Queen of Scots and Princess Wilhelmine of Prussia, many among the royalty applied their talents to classical forms, especially baroque. It would be some time before the stringed instrument became linked with folk.

In Ireland, a long line of harp-composers flourished, perhaps starting around A.D. 1000 (a true date is impossible to pinpoint) and stretching to 1800. These were professional musicians who traveled the countryside plying their trade to patrons for special celebrations. While some became well known, including Turlough O'Carolan and Denis O'Hampsey, many toiled in obscurity, because their efforts were never documented.

The fiddle became a genuine folk music instrument. The modern European violin evolved from various stringed instruments that arrived from other countries. In China it was the erhu, in Southeast Asia it was the rebab and in India it was the esraj. In the late Renaissance, centered in Italy, the violin's improved tone, agility, and volume, and its easy portability made it ideal for the traveling musician. Its popularity spread through Europe, especially in Ireland, England and Scotland, where Niel Gow would dominate for decades with his unique sound.

In the eighteenth century, the first accordion appeared and rapidly spread through Russia, South America, North America and Europe. Because of its versatility, a solo performer was able to sound like an entire group. The accordion would play a large role in the preservation and extension of ethnic music.

Other instruments such as the banjo, dulcimer and bass would be much later additions, introduced in the Appalachian region. There were a number of different bells, whistles, and stringed inventions in the early centuries, but none of them had a significant impact. The harmonica would occupy its own special place in the development of the folk genre. The harmonica player would often accompany himself on the guitar. The French harp was also small, and another portable musical instrument perfect for the traveling folkies.

In the twentieth century, the dominant folk instrument was the acoustic guitar. The six-string music box has a long and colorful history, first emerging in Spain, where it was utilized for classical duty. Throughout the centuries it underwent many changes at the hands of different cultures. Interestingly, despite the advancements and popularization of the solid electric model, the folkies were much more enthusiastic about the acoustic version.

Once the composers and musicians had made their mark in folk music, a wealth of material needed to be carefully preserved. Collectors began to assemble the old airs into some cohesive order. The first collectors were ethnomusicologists and musicologists long before the term was coined. Their foresight in appreciating history was crucial in keeping the music alive. Collecting spread throughout the world, as each country had a school of serious students.

The historical figures in this book are a merely a handful of dozens who made an impact on folk music in a variety of roles, as musicians, composers and collectors. Some figures not included in this book are A. Martin Freeman, Abdessadeq Cheqara, Adam de la Halle, Charles Dibdin, Anders Blomquist, Canon James Goodman, Daniel Emmett, John Edward Pigot, Thomas More, and Sir John Stevenson, among others.

Thomas D'Urfey was the first composer to make a scant living from writing early folk material. He also penned plays.

Turlough O'Carolan was an Irish harp master whose music continues to be relevant to this day.

Denis O'Hampsey was another harp musician who kept the old style alive more than any of his fellow musicians.

Edward Bunting provided invaluable information on the harp masters, including O'Carolan and O'Hampsey, among others.

Targjei Augundsson is the father of Norwegian folk and did much to preserve the music in his country and surrounding Northern European nations.

Ostap Versai was a Ukrainian kobzar (bard) who had a deep impact on modern folk.

Francis J. Child was an important collector whose five-volume work continues to influence scholars.

Niel Gow was a Scottish fiddler who became the dominant musician of his era. He inspired generations of his own family and others to follow in his footsteps.

Cecil Sharp has been dubbed the founding father of the folklore revival in England in the early twentieth century. His work reverberated throughout the century.

Thomas D'Urfey (1653–1723)
English Folk Comic

The evolution of songwriting is long, distinguished and very interesting. Many of the earliest tunesmiths wrote material in order to gain favor with the monarchy, while simultaneously trying to please the average citizen, which provided a true challenge. One individual rose to the occasion and entertained both the royalty and peasantry with his funny, common folk songs. His name was Thomas D'Urfey.

D'Urfey was born in 1653 in Devonshire, England. Some family histories claimed him as a descendant of Honoré d'Urfé, a noted French author. Perhaps he was related to the famous writer. It was also suggested that he was descended from the ill-fated Huguenots, but proper documentation was never provided and the claim was suspect.

Young Thomas stuttered and it seemed as if he would suffer a life of hardship and poverty in the class-driven English society of the day. Initially, D'Urfey was trained in the law and was possibly a scrivener's apprentice. However, he discovered a love of songs, especially the interplay of words. His facility with words would serve him well throughout his life. He began a long apprenticeship to become a writer, which initially seemed a dream.

He became a playwright. In 1676, his first staged production, *The Siege of Memphis,* was a critical and financial failure. But D'Urfey, not to be deterred easily, continued to improve his writing and turned his attention to humor. A few months later he returned with the comedy *Madam Fickle,* which was a success with both the monarchy and the common folk. It impressed Charles II and the Duke of Ormonde, enabling D'Urfey to secure the favors of the king, an achievement every writer of his day hoped to attain.

The successful playwright evolved into a witty, satirical author of clever, bawdy folk tunes. He accompanied himself on the lute and developed a knack for pouring out this material and presenting it in a way which engaged the audience without offending any of the well-respected patrons. D'Urfey became a kind of musical court jester to wealthy patrons and every monarch who occupied the throne. Except for a brief stint as a music teacher at a girls' school, he worked for the upper class of English society throughout the rest of his career.

Although he was not a wealthy performer, D'Urfey often traveled to his venues accompanied by a page. In 1683, in a further attempt to appear to be of a higher social class, he added an apostrophe to his name, and probably came up with the false family history claims.

By this time, D'Urfey's career was balanced between well-known songwriter and playwright. Often, he combined the two, inserting his music into his plays. He collected songs and ballads in *Wit and Mirth or Pills to Purge Melancholy.* While his stage work was well-received, the saucy, vulgar tunes were discarded as rubbish, although such ditties as "The Fart; Famous for Its Satyrical Humour in the Reign of Queen Anne" proved to be an underground favorite.

The creation of such suggestive material led to his greatest contribution to the English theater: the ballad opera. These compositions combined racy and satirical dialogue with characters who were often of the criminal element. John Gay's *The Beggar's Opera* was the most famous of this type of theater piece and contained at least ten of D'Urfey's songs. The classic piece remains popular to this day.

D'Urfey continued to produce bawdy songs, plays and poems until the time of his death. On February 26, 1723, one of the first songwriters to make a living at the trade passed away. Three years later a fitting epitaph was erected which glorified his skill as a comic, a wit and one of the driving forces behind the ballad opera.

Thomas D'Urfey was one of the earliest celebrated folksong poets. He possessed an array of compositional skills and although he never became wealthy, he earned enough to enjoy a decent life. The range of his work included political ditties, satires, country and court songs, as well as the first ballad operas. The author of more than 500 songs and 32 plays was a true wordsmith.

A partial list of D'Urfey's songs includes "Sometimes I Am a Tapster New," "Honest Shepherd Since You're Poor," "Blowzabella My Bouncing Doxie," "There Was a Lass of Islington," "Poor Celia Once Was Very Fair," "What Life Can Compare with the Jolly Town Rake's," "Would Ye Have a Young Virgin of Fifteen Years," "Weep All Ye Nymphs, Your Floods Unbind," "A Soldier and a Sailor, a Tinker and a Taylor," "How Vile Are the Sordid Intrigues of the Town," "Like a Ring Without a Finger," "There Was an Old Woman Liv'd Under a Hill," "Oh! My Panting, Panting Heart," "Do Not Rumple My Top-knot," and "Come Jug My Honey, Let's to Bed."

His facility with words enabled him to cover a wide range of material and create a repertoire with proper songs for different audiences. The court songs charmed royalty, while his country songs were coarse and dealt with the life of the common English folk. The political material celebrated those in authority, praising their greatness rather than criticizing their mistakes and faults.

As a songwriter, D'Urfey was not cut in the mold of a Stephen Foster. However, he had an indirect link with later, politically active folksingers like Woody Guthrie, Lee Hays, Cisco Houston and Pete Seeger. Modern novelty writers and writers of bawdy songs can trace their origins to the English comic.

D'Urfey was a marginally talented musician whose strength was in the interplay, wit and charm of the words he put together. Therefore a number of composers put his lyrics to music, including Henry Purcell, Dr. John Blow, and John Eccles, among others. That a number of different composers were able to use his humorous, satirical lyrics indicates a tremendous versatility in his writing.

Although many disapproved of the vulgar nature of D'Urfey's songs, they still sang them. Meanwhile, he continued to write plays and poetry in order to be taken seriously. While some of the common folk thought of his work as drivel, others such as essayists Richard Steele and Joseph Addison, considered him a true contemporary. Alexander Pope, one of the greatest English poets of his or any generation and a first-class satirist, also praised D'Urfey.

D'Urfey's plays include *The Siege of Memphis*; *Madam Fickle*; *The Fond Husband*; *The Virtuous Wife*; *Wonders in the Sun, or, The Kingdom of the Birds*;

The Campaigners; The Love of Money; Sir Courtly Nice; The Banditti; The Bath; A Common-Wealth of Women; The Comical History of Don Quixote; The Comical History of Don Quixote, Part II; The Comical History of Don Quixote, Part III; The Fool Turn'd Critick; A Fool's Preferment; The Intrigues at Versailles; Love for Money; The Marriage-Hater Match'd; The Modern Prophets; The Old Mode & the New; The Richmond Heiress; The Rise and Fall of Massaniello; The Rise and Fall of Massaniello, Part II; The Royalist, Sir Barnaby Whigg; Squire Oldsapp; Trick for Trick; and *The Injured Princess*, among others. Many of these were forerunners to the ballad opera and enjoyed a solid staging in various British theaters.

Although not considered a great bard on the level of Shakespeare or Ben Jonson, D'Urfey published poetry during his lifetime. One of his works, the multi-volume, *Wit and Mirth or Pills to Purge Melancholy*, included songs and ballads. Because of his foresight in capturing the spirit of England, he was later considered a historian and a true patriot.

Thomas D'Urfey was a good writer with a gift for the witty, the satirical, the bawdy. The elements found in his work had an indirect influence on some modern folk material. Because of the genius of his compositions, the contributions of the English folk comic have not been forgotten.

Turlough O'Carolan (1670–1738)
The Gaelic Harpist

Although every country has its own brand of folk music, there is a general consensus that Ireland was the cradle of the current modern Anglo-American style. There were pipers, harpers, fiddlers and singers who plied their trade in the bustling cities and throughout the vast countryside. The harp players were the strongest contingent, including the man considered the last great Gaelic harpist. His name was Turlough O'Carolan.

O'Carolan was born in 1670, near Nobber, County Meath, and later moved to Ballyfarnan, County Roscommon. His father secured employment with the notable MacDermott Roe family and the lady of the house took a shine to young Turlough. She provided the ambitious boy with an education that allowed him to develop his gift for poetry. In his late teens, a bout of smallpox left him blind, and his life suddenly took a much different path. O'Carolan studied the harp with the hope of becoming an itinerant musician.

In 1692, he began his career. As a spirited poet/musician, he journeyed through the Irish countryside and composed songs for patrons. He spent time in the houses of the Irish gentry, where he was well fed. He drank the best whiskeys and performed a number or two in honor of the host. He became very good at the vocation and had a facility in composing lyrics on the spot to celebrate special occasions. O'Carolan built an incredible reputation, and legend recounts that ceremonies such as weddings, birthdays and funerals were stalled until his arrival.

In the early eighteenth century, O'Carolan heard some Italian baroque music at a nobleman's home and incorporated some of its elements into his own style. But he could never become a baroque composer because of his blindness, which kept him from studying harmony, counterpoint, and musical form. In addition, the Irish harp, being diatonic, like a piano with white keys only, was incapable of playing highbrow music with its accidentals and key changes. Still, from this point on, the tunes Turlough composed comprised a delightful mixture of folk and classical elements.

Most traditional Irish songs usually have two repeating sections of equal length. In O'Carolan's music, though, the second sections were often longer than the first, and were extended by unusual melodic twists and turns as he attempted to give his compositions a baroque sound. This also set his style apart from those of the other harpist-poets.

In 1720, O'Carolan married Mary Maguire, a girl much younger than his 50 years. Their family in Mohill, County Leitrim, included seven children, one boy and six girls. By this time he was well established in his career as a wandering minstrel and was able to provide for a large family. In 1733, Mary passed away.

In 1726, the harper's music was first published in John and William Neale's *A Collection of the Most Celebrated Irish Tunes*, which provided a glimpse into O'Carolan's creativity. The hundreds of songs later attributed to the great Irish minstrel cannot be assigned to him for certain because many were passed down orally through the repertoires of fiddlers, pipers and Irish harpists several generations removed from O'Carolan's era.

On March 25, 1738, after more than half a century performing as a traveling musician/poet, he passed away. He was buried in the village of Keadue, County Roscommon. Nearly 300 years later the annual O'Carolan Harp Festival and Summer School commemorates his life and work at his burial spot, ensuring that the harpist-poet master is not forgotten.

Turlough O'Carolan was a powerful itinerant Irish musician. Even during his life he was accorded widespread fame and his legend has only grown over the centuries. He was a composer and singer of great delicacy and is considered by many to be Ireland's national composer. He had a particular touch and was able to transmit this magic through his music.

O'Carolan possessed an incomparable gift for melodic composition and it was this ability upon which his fame was built. This divine skill enabled him to remain dominant in successive generations, while most of Turlough's contemporaries faded into obscurity, despite doubts about the authorship of some music attributed to him.

O'Carolan called each of his compositions a "planxty," a term which nearly 300 years later continues to cause controversy. Some believe it to be a song composed in honor of a specific person, however, others say that "planxty" was a word created by those documenting the Irish harpist's catalog. Some cynics strongly believe that O'Carolan invented the term himself to confuse future historians. The latter is a possibility, because it is evident that he was a clever individual with a vivid imagination.

Unfortunately, because much of his work is legendary, the exact events of his lifetime are uncertain. Without recordings and documentation, the extent of his authorship of songs credited to him is also uncertain. Many Irish tunes were in the public domain, and much of the material was recycled to fit specific needs.

An Irish patriot, O'Carolan wrote the majority of credited material in his native tongue. He used original material and borrowed from older, traditional melodies that he lengthened and changed to suit his needs. The harpist also listened carefully to the songs of rivals and was able to improvise and improve upon them.

During his more than 50-year career as a traveling minstrel, Turlough created songs of love, joy, remembrance, happiness, sorrow and every emotion in the human spectrum on a whim, according to eyewitnesses. The master poet's brain was an encyclopedia of stored melodies, harmonies and lyrics which he could instantly rework into one coherent package to satisfy a specific patron.

It wasn't until the latter part of the nineteenth century that his work was gathered piecemeal in a serious collection, but many of the lyrics were missing. O'Carolan probably recycled many of his best phrases to serve in more than one song. This may have made recording the lyrics problematic.

In 1958, two centuries after his death, his entire repertoire was published in one edition, *Carolan—The Life, Times, and Music of an Irish Harper*. Editor Donal O'Sullivan did a remarkable job. However the few lyrics that appeared disappointed many critics. A different book, *The Bunting Collection of Irish Folk Music and Song*, also by O'Sullivan, appeared some time later and inspired a new interest in O'Carolan's music.

Because harpists always relied on their memories to preserve songs, many of the compositions of the seventeenth and eighteenth centuries were lost. However, some of Turlough's material was included in the repertoire of contemporary harpists who lived into the early eighteenth century, including Arthur O'Neill, Patrick Quin and Denis O'Hampsey. The oral tradition allowed many of O'Carolan's compositions to survive.

Some of the tunes credited to O'Carolan include "O'Carolan's Concerto," "Lord Inchiqin," "Betty MacNeill," "Athlone," "Elizabeth MacDermott Roe," "Kean O'Hara," "Brian MaGuire," "Major Shanly," "Merry Maids of Connaught," "Lament for Sir Ulick Burke, "O'Carolan's Favorite Jig," "George Brabazon, 1st Air," and "Dr. John Hart, Bishop of Achonry." In all, more than 200 songs have been attributed to him, although their authenticity is a point scholars continue to debate.

A number of his compositions have remained popular and are performed by modern groups including Planxty, the Chieftains and the Dubliners. Derek Bell, the harper for the Chieftains, made a solo recording entitled *Carolan's Receipt*. Fingerstyle guitarists also discovered this rich musical vein, including Eric Schoenberg, a well known Celtic figure. O'Carolan influenced hundreds of Irish singers and musicians to the point that almost all of them have begun their musical careers with one of his tunes, especially the classic, "Elizabeth MacDermott Roe." Even the Foot Guards of the British Army have delved into the harpist-poet's songbook.

Turlough O'Carolan was an Irish musical jewel. For nearly 50 years he plied the trade which made him famous and kept him so long after he had passed away. The depth of the minstrel's popularity can be measured in several ways: he was depicted on the £50 note in the Republic of Ireland, and Keadue, County Roscommon, where he is buried, is the site of the annual O'Carolan Harp Festival and Summer School that celebrates the harpist's life and work. A plaque in St. Patrick's Cathedral in Dublin declares that he was the last of the Irish bards. The Gaelic harpist indeed left a mark on the people of Ireland as well as throughout the world.

Denis O'Hampsey (1695–1807)

Harp Magic

From A.D. 1000 to A.D. 1800, the main musical instrument in Ireland was the harp. The country produced numerous practitioners of the folk tradition. While many were deft, a select few were as truly gifted as one man renowned for his harp magic. His name was Denis O'Hampsey.

O'Hampsey was born in 1695, in Craigmore, near Garvagh County Derry, Ireland. However, his parents were both from Magilligan, a village northwest of his birth place, and it was here that Denis grew up. When he was three, tragedy struck. A bout with smallpox claimed his eyesight. Despite this obstacle, the young boy attempted to make something of himself.

The folk music of his people filled the air. This caught O'Hampsey's attention and imagination. He explored the possibilities of the harp and quickly developed a deft touch, so that he became a first-rate player able to make a living as a musician. A blind person in the eighteenth century had very few employment opportunities, so a career as a harpist was a solid chance at a decent life.

At the age of twelve, he started formal study of the harp and through the devoted instruction of four different teachers, O'Hampsey blossomed into an excellent musician. Each instructor taught him something to build on and by his early twenties the aspiring artist was ready to set out and make a living as an itinerant musician.

The harpists in Ireland at the time followed two different styles. The majority cut their nails. But O'Hampsey kept his fingernails long and ragged, which enabled him to coax a fuller range of expression from his Gaelic harp. This style dated back to the earliest of times and he became one of the last practitioners of the ancient tradition.

The blind poet/musician traveled the Irish countryside entertaining various patrons with his fine musical skills. He was blessed with an ability to compose tunes from an encyclopedia of remembered harmonies, melodies and lyrics. With a facility for words, the minstrel was able to assemble songs to fit each occasion and client.

O'Hampsey was also a collector. He possessed an excellent memory which allowed him to retain a wealth of original and traditional tunes. As well as his own material, the harpist managed to preserve old, cherished Irish airs, odes, and planxties.

O'Hampsey expanded his territory with sojourns into Scotland, which proved to be very successful. These trips allowed him to add Scottish songs of all types to his growing repertoire of folk material. Upon his return home, he passed what he had learned on his voyages to fellow musicians, thus preserving among them a wider range of material.

O'Hampsey, like his contemporary, O'Carolan, performed for the Irish gentry as well as the common people and wrote songs about them titled with their names. His inventiveness made him a favorite at weddings and other celebrations. His cleverness endeared him to his patrons. In 1747, he greatly enhanced his reputation when he performed for the son of Prince Charles Stuart. This became one of the high points of his long, distinguished career.

In eighteenth century Ireland, harpists were admired for many different reasons. They were considered magicians, with their ability to pluck the strings and draw magic airs from them. The Irish were a downtrodden people, fighting bitterly against the English for control of their country, and tunesmiths like O'Hampsey helped raise the spirits of the people.

A creative individual, he would eventually be credited with the song

"Robin Adair," one of the most beloved Irish tunes in a very large catalog. Various historical studies indicate that O'Hampsey used parts of several other songs to create his signature tune. This practice of borrowing from traditional tunes was standard at that time.

When he composed the song, contemporary harpists named it "Eileen Aroon," but eventually it evolved into its better known title. O'Hampsey had traveled throughout the Scottish countryside, where he often sang the original version. When the native Highland minstrels heard the enchanting piece, they learned it and changed the structure. It became "Robin Adair." Although he had composed hundreds of songs over his career, it became his signature tune.

In 1792, O'Hampsey arrived at the Belfast Harp Festival, where young musicologist Edward Bunting interviewed him. It was an event of significant historical importance for Irish folk music. The old master proved that he was a legitimate contender among the greatest harpists in the history of the instrument.

In a time when such documentation was rare, Bunting's interview was vitally important. The festival was not only a showcase for the musicians but also provided a glimpse into the daily life of the average Irish citizen. Many came to hear their favorite harpist perform, in most cases O'Hampsey, who would deliver his magic songs in a completely different setting than his usual.

For decades, he traveled the pathways and roads of the Irish and Scottish countryside to entertain the patrons. The harp master was a welcomed and recognized personage, as integral to the landscape as brooks, flowers, forests, and churches. Eventually, O'Hampsey retired from minstrel work and settled in Magilligan, where his parents had land holdings. He died in November 1807, at the ripe old age of 112.

Denis O'Hampsey was another of Ireland's musical jewels. He was an important piece of the patchwork of Ireland's folk sound. His harp skills were equal to any who had come before and superior to those of his contemporaries. The old master's music remains relevant to this day as it continues to influence aspiring harpists.

O'Hampsey played a cherished "Queen Mary" harp with strings made of brass, silver or gold, a tradition among harpists from the beginning of the millennium through the middle ages. O'Carolan also performed on this type of instrument on occasion, but the practice would die out in the early nineteenth century, making O'Hampsey one of the last such performers.

O'Hampsey influenced many harp players in Ireland and around the world. A short list includes Thomas Connellan, William Connellan, Cormac de Barra, Órla Fallon, Piaras Feiritéar, Geraldine McMahon, Katie McMahon, Áine Minogue, Mary O'Hara, and Claire Roche, among others. Many harpists start their apprenticeship with his catalog.

O'Hampsey was paid to perform at celebrations and once he was well established, there was great demand for his services. Although he is credited with creating only one song, he performed hundreds of them for different patrons. Some of his best known songs include: "Lady Letitia Burke," "Burns' March," "An Chúilfhionn" (Coolin or Lady of the Desert), "Brighid na bPéarlaidh" (Bridget of the Pearls), "A Mhuirnín" (The Darling; literally "My Darling"), "Eirghe An Lae" (Dawn of Day), "Sin Sios Suas Liom" (Down Beside Me), "Eibhlín a Rúin" (Eileen Aroon), "Coladh an tSionnaigh," (The Fox's Sleep), "A chailíní, a' bhfaca sibh Seóirse" (Girls, Have You Seen George or Conor Macareavy), "Tá mé i mo chodhladh is ná dúisigh mé" (I Am Asleep and Don't Waken Me), "The Jointure," "John Jones," "Bob Jordan," "Madam Keel or Eleanor Plunkett," "A Lovely Lass to a Friar Came," "Love Is a Tormenting Pain or Showers of Rain," "Planxty Connor," "Kitty O'Hara," "Maidin Bheag Aoibhinn" (Soft Mild Morning), "Mailí San Seórse" (Molly St. George), "Uilleagán Dubh O" (literally, Dark Head O [The Song of Sorrow], "Tá an samhradh ag teacht" (Summer Is Coming), "Féach an gléas" (Try If It Is in Tune), "Ceann Dubh Dilis" (Black Headed Deary), "The King Shall Enjoy His Own Again," "Molly Bheag O" (Little Molly O), "The White Cockade," "Molly Stuart," "Hob Nob," "The Dying Lover," and "Saibha gheal ni Granda."

Among the most fertile venues for O'Hampsey were the annual musical gatherings. At these events he dazzled everyone from attendees to fellow musicians with his expertise, and often showed up very skilled younger players. It was at the Belfast Harp Festival where his work as well as his words were transcribed for history, which assured him an important place in folklore.

O'Hampsey was the last of the traditional Gaelic harpers. His death marked the beginning of a low period for the instrument, which would not enjoy a renaissance until decades later, when harpists turned to the master's catalog for inspiration. Many scholars believe his true legacy was a personal effort to ensure that the Downhill harp he played survived for future generations. Through interviews, O'Hampsey passed on the techniques, repertoire and style for the coveted harp.

For over two centuries, musical scholars have studied the life of one of Ireland's greatest harpists. Many aspects of his career have been celebrated because of its richness and diversity. With each new discovery, his legend grows and shines. O'Hampsey represents an important part of history and the Irish people have not forgotten his contributions.

Denis O'Hampsey was an interesting figure who did much to continue the ancient tradition of the Irish harp. On the occasion of the two hundredth anniversary of his death, there was a grand celebration of his life and music in County Derry and in Dundee and Fife, Scotland. Undoubtedly, O'Hampsey had a special touch — harp magic.

Niel Gow (1727–1807)

Scottish Fiddle Dance Master

The fiddle, harp and lute were the dominant instruments in the early years of folk music, and each different region of many European countries boasted a champion. In Scotland, the fiddler was a revered individual and a source of national pride. In the eighteenth century, one individual attained considerable fame because of the fire and imagination he possessed as a fiddle dance master. His name was Niel Gow.

Gow was born in 1727, in Inver, Perthshire. He discovered the fiddle at a very young age and taught himself some of the basics. At thirteen, the blossoming musician studied under a formal teacher for a few years before deciding that he could not make a living at music. He trained to be a plaid weaver. For some time, the teenager worked at the trade, but music was in his blood, and he returned to the fiddle full time.

While still in his teens, the aspiring artist caught his first big break when he entered a competition and won. The judge, John McKaw, a blind musician of considerable fame, praised Gow's ability on the fiddle. The attention provided many opportunities and the determined young man made the most of them, accepting all work that came his way and impressing everyone with his formidable skills. The virtuoso excelled at every venue.

In 1744, the Duke of Atholl was impressed enough to become Gow's patron. From this point on, the young fiddler found permanent work playing for balls and dance parties attended by the local nobility. His reputation grew to near legendary status with each successive performance and he surpassed all competitors. That he was able to entertain the wealthy as well as the common peasant was a tribute to his versatility.

Gow married a local girl who bore him eight children. His son Nathaniel was a fine composer of nearly 200 Scottish tunes. Others became musicians while a couple of his offspring sold music. The family became one of the most prominent in entertainment circles. Its reputation would extend into the nineteenth century.

The death of his first wife caused a depression so strong that he lost the desire to play. He put down his instrument, to the chagrin of those who enjoyed his music so much, and returned to work as a plaid weaver. The famous fiddle responsible for entertaining so many remained silent for some time.

In 1768, he remarried and found happiness again. A desire to continue to entertain and the pleading of his rather large fan base coaxed him into picking up the fiddle once again. Gow played at the old venues to the delight of those who had missed his supreme talent. Sadly, the second phase of his career was cut short due to illness. On March 1, 1807, the great Scottish musician passed away at the age of 80.

Niel Gow was an important Scottish fiddler. Many historians consider him to be the best the country produced during the eighteenth century, remarkable considering the number of other musicians who plied their trade during that time span. His reputation as a fiddle dance master was well earned. He had a superior ability on the instrument that was constantly challenged, but rarely matched.

He could race along with lively jigs that truly moved a crowd, and slow the pace for the romantic interludes that couples enjoyed so much. Gow used a wide range of material including hot rural folk dance tunes, classical numbers, ditties, historical pieces and his own clever compositions. The speed, dexterity and precision of each provided the foundation of his fame.

His greatest skill as a fiddler was in his bowing techniques, which separated him from all the other players. He tried different ways of drawing sound from the instrument that contemporaries never could duplicate, much less master. Gow had a powerful and unique approach, and his special touches placed him in a category all by himself.

Perhaps one of the most striking features of Gow's original material was its strong Scottish flavor. The patriotic fiddler believed in the struggle of his people and this was reflected in his music, which was one reason home audiences loved him. His nationalistic sensitivity continues to reverberate among Scotland's folk performers.

Gow is credited with nearly 90 songs, which remain the backbone of the Scottish country dance catalog to this day. He drew inspiration from his own experience to create songs from the people he knew, family experiences and observations of life of the good people from the homeland. There was an artistry in his compositions that also boasted a universal experience. Because of this, they survived the test of time.

Although a brilliant original composer, Gow was not above borrowing from others. Perhaps as much as a quarter of the master fiddler's songs were taken from other musicians and reworked into something new and fresh. This was common practice during the era and others borrowed from Gow's original work as much as he did from them.

Some of the songs he played at dances and balls were taken from old material popular in Scotland for years. Thus he preserved Scotland's musical heritage by playing the ancient tunes so they would not be forgotten, and he kept them fresh in the audience's mind. Some of the songs he kept intact while others he updated to serve and entertain a modern, eighteenth-century crowd.

Niel Gow played many different types of tunes. One lament was titled "Neil Gow's Lament for the Death of His Second Wife." He also wrote jigs like "The Stool of Repentance," as well as reels like "Dunkeld Bridge," "Farewell to Whisky," and "Miss McLeod's Reel." He also penned measures such as "Lady Mary Hay's Scotch Measure." He was famous for his strathspeys, including "Highland Whisky," "Lady Madelina Sinclair," "Loch Ericht Side," "Miss Drummond of Perth's Strathspey," "Miss Stewart of Grantully's Strathspey" and "Mr. Moray of Abercairny."

Many of Gow's tunes inspired the Scottish poet Robert Burns. The bard was greatly impressed with the native fiddler and often complimented his music in public, which only enhanced the musician's already sterling reputation. Later Burns would visit Gow, one of his favorite artists, to acknowledge his hearty, simple, robust accomplishments.

During his lifetime, two great collections of Gow's work were published. The first, in 1784, was called *A Collection of Strathspey Reels*. The second was entitled *Complete Repository of Original Scots Slow Strathspeys and Dances*. These works influenced generations of fiddlers throughout Scotland, England, Ireland and other countries.

Because of the Duke of Atholl's patronage, Gow was exposed to much of the upper crust of English society. Although the simple fiddler had very little in common with the nobility, the gentry greatly admired his ability. He played for other members of Europe's ruling class, including the Duchess of Gordon, who also became Gow's patron. No matter who the audience, his sound remained simple and provincial. Gow had the cleverness to play in a rural tradition while catering to noble sensibilities.

The dance master was not only the most important Scottish fiddler of the eighteenth century, he also spawned a family tradition. His children would, like their father, elevate the traditional folk music of their land to greater heights. All those who followed him built on his reputation of excellence. The Gows became the first family of the country dance in Scotland.

In the beginning, Gow often played solo, but once his children were old enough, they joined him to perform at Highland weddings and balls. On occasion, Gow's brother also joined the outfit. Despite the number of musicians in the group, the master fiddler was always the leader and often stood out because he had more talent than any of the others.

Gow was on the scene at an opportune time. After the English defeat of the Scottish at Culloden in 1746, the crown directed suppressive measures against the Scottish people. One law forbade possession of a weapon. A bagpipe was considered a weapon, while the fiddle was not. From this point on, the fiddlers thrived.

Even though he died more than 200 years ago, the people of Scotland have not forgotten one of their favorite sons. There is an annual Niel Gow Fiddle Festival that takes place in Dunkeld and Birnam, Perthshire, Scotland. It was established in 2004 to celebrate his life and music. Musicians from all over the land and from the international scene come to play during the spring event.

The painter Sir Henry Raeburn took it upon himself to produce many portraits of Gow during his lifetime as his fame spread widely throughout Scotland and England. The noted fiddler was a stout man who appeared to have powerful arms. Although they don't show in the many portraits, he seemed to have magic fingers. That Raeburn painted so many portraits of Gow underlines the respect he commanded during his prime.

Niel Gow was an admired entertainer throughout his career. He remains one of the best loved fiddlers Scotland ever produced. The master had a magic touch and wasn't afraid to experiment to give his music an edge over the competition. His exceptional talent, patriotic heart, wisdom to take advantage of opportunities, and the uncanny ability to please both nobility and peasant at once made him the Scottish fiddle dance master.

Edward Bunting (1773–1843)
The Transcriber

The rich, distinct folk music tradition of Ireland had existed for some time before it was diligently cataloged for posterity. To preserve it properly called for an individual with formal musical training as well as a keen sense of historical perspective. One person emerged to fill the role and because of his precise eye for detail became known as "the transcriber." His name was Edward Bunting.

Bunting was born in 1773, in County Armagh, Ireland. At seven, it was decided that he should begin a musical career and he was relocated to Drogheda to learn the craft. Bunting learned how to play the organ and read music and compose it. Four years later, he was sent to Belfast, where he apprenticed under William Ware, a noted organist at St. Anne's church.

In 1792, at the age of nineteen, Bunting was commissioned by the Belfast Harp Festival to transcribe the music of the oral-tradition players. Because he was a trained musician, he did not fully understand many of the techniques such as modes, and transcribed all the songs as though they were classical music. However, it was a successful endeavor because of the meticulous notes he took, the intelligent questions he asked and the personal interpretation he added that shed light on one of the greatest Irish traditions. That day, the young musicologist established himself as the prime folklorist of Ireland, especially with his in-depth interview of the famous harp master Denis O'Hampsey.

From 1792 to 1807, Bunting would conduct many of these collecting tours. He often transcribed songs while the musicians were performing, which meant he captured the freshness, authenticity and expressive weight of the old folk tunes. With his acute ear and deep musical knowledge, he was able to provide an accurate record of the cherished material. In 1796, his first scholarly work, *A General Collection of the Ancient Irish Music,* which included 66 tunes, was published.

In 1809, a second volume entitled *A General Collection of the Ancient Music of Ireland* appeared. In 1819, Bunting married and moved to Dublin, where he found work as the organist at St. George's Church. During this period, little was heard from the scholarly music master because he was busy transcribing the many notes he had taken during his festival excursions. Moreover, his duties at the church and family obligations occupied most of his time.

In 1840, he resurfaced with *The Ancient Music of Ireland.* It included more than 150 tunes and a dissertation on the Irish harp and harpists, as well as an account of the old melodies of Ireland. This scholarly work would be studied for decades after its publication.

In the preface of the third collection, Bunting described the Belfast Harp Festival and defended the need to preserve the history of Irish music. The tunes which had changed little from one generation to another provided a glimpse of life in Ireland through the years. His foresight in realizing the importance of maintaining a record of folksongs guaranteed his place in history.

The work shed light on the entire Irish musical tradition. Very ancient pieces, mostly dirges, had survived through the oral tradition, tunes which harpists such as O'Hampsey and O'Carolan had heard through their travels.

In the second part of his scholarly work were the ancient tunes often accompanied by words, sometimes more modern versions of older songs. The words opened a window onto the age of the pieces. The time-honored airs were often attributed to composers, including Lyons, Daly, Connellan, and O'Cahan.

The third section demonstrated a definite progression from the very ancient songs. Once again he demonstrated improvements or new takes on older tunes. It also spoke of outside influences, particularly Italian opera, that diluted the pure Irish product. Bunting's opinions gave the book an excellent personal insight which greatly enhanced the entire dissertation.

The book was also interesting on another front because it included the names of all those who attended the 1792 Belfast Harp Festival and introduced the most famous harpists of the day. The list included Dennis O'Hampsey (or Hempson, as was recorded), Arthur O'Neill, Charles Fanning, Daniel Black, Charles Byrne, Hugh Higgins, Patrick Quin, William

Carr, Rose Mooney and James Duncan. It also mentions the Welsh harper William Williams.

Bunting enjoyed a strong career and was instrumental in maintaining interest in Irish folk music. His ability to document the history and importance of festivals earned him a reputation as a noted musicologist. On December 21, 1843, three years after his last collection was published, he died. He was buried in Dublin.

Edward Bunting was an Irish musicologist long before the term had been defined. His contribution to the preservation of the tunes of his native country was crucial to their survival. But more than that, he gave the musical community a personal insight into the grand tradition of the harpists of Ireland.

Bunting's first volume, *A General Collection of the Ancient Music of Ireland,* set the tone for what would follow. His effort celebrated a tradition that had existed for over eight hundred years, at a time when the great harpist culture was fading, before it enjoyed a renaissance later in the century. The tradition continues to flourish and directly benefited from Edward's scholarly works.

Since Bunting's collections there have been others, however over a hundred years would elapse before the next one, Charlotte Milligan Fox's *Annals of the Irish Harpers.* Various volumes would follow, including Henry Lewis's *Musica: British Museum Additional Manuscript.* Although both were scholarly works, neither had the insight and historical value of Bunting's effort.

Bunting was credited with preserving an integral piece of Irish history with his biographical notes, careful attention to detail of the terminology used, and most importantly, rescue of hundreds of songs that would have been lost forever. He was in many ways the first musicologist and ethnomusicologist, years before the term was coined. Although he was commissioned to appear at the festival, Bunting's enthusiasm for the project put him in a special category.

In 1807, a Miss Owenson, also known as Lady Morgan, published *The Wild Irish Girl: A National Tale.* The book was published before Bunting's work and it included details about Arthur O'Neill's harp, as well as an excerpt about Denis O'Hampsey's life. But it lacked the precise details of *A General Collection of the Ancient Music of Ireland.*

In 1792, when Bunting interviewed Arthur O'Neill, Charles Fanning, Daniel Black, Charles Byrne, Hugh Higgins, Denis O'Hampsey, Patrick Quin, William Carr, Rose Mooney and James Duncan, he helped the careers of these struggling musicians. In that era, there were few opportunities for musicians to expand their career through media resources.

Edward Bunting was an exceptional scholar who devoted his life to the preservation of the precise historical tradition of the Irish harpists. His precedent-setting work glorified the world of these important musicians and enabled them to gain greater support in the community. The three volumes of his work were a grand effort and earned him the title of the transcriber.

Targjei Augundsson (1801–1872)
Father of Norwegian Folk

Each country has its own folk music, and most boast one individual who is regarded as the founder of the national sound. In Norway, the folk tradition had existed for centuries, but one figure brought everything together. In the process he would earn the title of "Father of Norwegian Folk" for his efforts. His name was Targjei Augundsson.

Augundsson was born in 1801, in Sauherad, Norway. His father was a serf and farmer as well as a country fiddler. The boy, better known as Myllarguten (which means "Millerboy," a name he picked up while working at a mill), took up the fiddle on the sly. When the father heard his son play, he was astonished at the youth's natural skill and determined that the youth would get the best teachers.

Augundsson would learn much from various teachers including champion fiddler Knut Lurås, who taught the aspiring musician work ethic, endurance, and pride. Øystein Langedrag, a soldier, played in a military style which had a tremendous influence on Augundsson. Augundsson rounded out his sound to become an excellent player and embarked on a lifelong career.

One of the most important aspects of Augundsson's music was his competitive spirit. Throughout his lifetime, Lurås and Håvard Gibøen would be among his main rivals, and he often battled them for supremacy. Although Augundsson would be a very harsh critic of others, he regarded his two main rivals as his near equals. In concert, inflammatory comments often fuelled the fire among the players.

Augundsson settled down in Telemark and made a life for himself there. He married and had a good number of children, including four sons who played the fiddle. Augundsson traveled far and wide performing at weddings as well as county feasts. He expanded his reputation in several of the small towns around the countryside.

He remained popular in various towns because of his ability to adapt dance-tunes he heard at various events into his own personal style. Augundsson also approached the art of fiddle playing differently than other musicians. Most musicians played short, crisp numbers, but Augundsson reinvented them, embellishing their thin melodies and lengthening them to give dancers more time on the floor, increasing their enjoyment. This innovation caught on in Telemark, then in other towns around Norway, and then in other Northern European centers.

Although Augundsson had established his fame in Telemark and abroad, the reigning champion of the fiddle in Norway at that time was Ole Bornemann Bull, the country's first genuine international star. However, he was more of a classical performer, while Augundsson had a stronger country flavor. As they simultaneously plied their trade in their respective venues, it was inevitable that they would someday meet.

In 1831, Augundsson and Ole Bull met and came away with a great respect for each other. Bull would include country folk tunes in his repertoire, which helped spread the music of Augundsson to a wider audience throughout Europe. While some critics dismissed Augundsson's work as local drivel, many were astonished that he was able to hold his own against the master, and also influence him so directly.

Many years later the two would perform together at a concert which served to enhance Augundsson's career. Although he was a solid fiddler, he never received the adulation that Bull enjoyed, which was often a genuine source of irritation. However, on this occasion, in a nervous fit, Augundsson played unscheduled material and his improvisational skills won over the audience. For one shining moment he stood alongside Bull as an equal in the eyes of everyone.

From the early 1840s on, Norway was swept up in a romantic nationalist fever, and the veteran musician enchanted all with his natural sounds. For the next few years he enjoyed the greatest surge of popularity of his entire career. In 1849, Augundsson and Ole Bull met one last time and they matched notes in front of a large audience. It was one of Augundsson's last great triumphs because when the nationalism died down, he was regarded as washed up, and he retired to work as a farmer.

The later years of his life were marked by depression, bitterness and loneliness. Throughout his career, Augundsson had made good money, but everything he had earned eventually evaporated, and on November 21, 1872, he died a pauper.

Augundsson was a genuine Norwegian national folk artist. He dedicated his life to the preservation of the rural tradition of his land and in the process became famous. Augundsson laid down the definitive style of folk fiddle playing which everyone after him copied and built upon. His influence has continued to the present time.

Augundsson's developed style was rooted in the traditional folk sound of Norway. His training and love of the country dance-tunes enabled him to channel the local idiom. His talent and wisdom allowed him to build on tradition in ways that would attract a greater audience.

His ability to change tunes and incorporate new ideas separated Augundsson from other players. The meeting with Ole Bull expanded his style and, arguably, made him a better musician. Most of his formerly rural repertoire took on a more classical sound after the encounter. Augundsson would learn to blend the two into one unique style which generations would learn and try to improve upon.

Augundsson's repertoire consisted of reinvented dance tunes picked up at local events. His ability to rework the tunes he heard into better material was his true artistic skill. He was able to take a few notes and create something new and exciting.

The speed, dexterity and precision of his playing was remarkable. He was capable of playing quick, furious, notey pieces which would exhaust even the strongest, most energetic dancers. Augundsson also performed slow numbers, melting the notes into a smooth run of comfortable sounds. The ability to change pace at a moment's notice was one of his hallmarks.

Details of Augundsson's life were somewhat lost in romantic lore. Stories about him, like his songs, were passed down orally from one generation to another. However, Rikard Berge, a noted folklorist, devoted much effort and time to collecting material in the late nineteenth century and early twentieth century to provide a more accurate picture of Augundsson and his contribution to Norwegian folk music.

Berge conducted many interviews with eyewitnesses to the crucial events which shaped Augundsson's life. He also questioned the fiddler's sons and closest intimates. The result was a fair portrait of a man with undeniable talent and a passion for folk dance-tunes played at a feverish pitch.

This biography and the tradition passed to younger musicians established Augundsson as the Father of Norwegian Music. A century later many still regarded him as a beacon, including Hallvard T. Bjørgum, Torleiv H. Bjørgum, Per Anders Buen Garnås, Knut Buen, Hauk Buen, Kristiane Lund, Andrea Een, Olav Jørgen Hegge, Vidar Lande, Annbjørg Lien, Lars Fykerud, Lars Jensen, Nils Økland and Kathryn Tickell. His influence spilled over the borders of Norway into the other Scandinavian countries.

There is a statue of Augundsson in his hometown of Telemark that many visit during special holidays, especially Norwegian Constitution Day on May 17. His music has been passed down from one generation to another and forms the bedrock of folk in Norway. Although the last few years of his life were difficult ones and he seemed to have been forgotten, only a handful of musicians have ever been accorded Augundsson's posthumous respect.

Augundsson was an important figure in the folk music of Norway. He kept the tradition alive and improved on technique, setting the precedent for future generations. He worked hard for this reputation and deserves to be called the Father of Norwegian Folk.

Ostap Veresai (1803–1899)

Ukrainian Minstrel

The folk artist has always been a versatile performer able to produce splendid versions of the country's traditional standards while also delivering something original. The first songwriters were capable of matching poetry to music and appealed to both the common man and the nobility. Many overcame incredible obstacles, including a musician known as the "Ukrainian minstrel." His name was Ostap Veresai.

Ostap Mykytovych Veresai was born in 1803, in the small village of Kaliuzhentsi, Pryluky County, into a musical family. His blind father was quite adept at the violin and made a meager living as an itinerant musician to support his family. At the age of four, Veresai lost his eyesight to illness.

Ukrainian kobzars, traveling musician-poets who played the bandora, a plucked string instrument similar to the oud, lute and guitar, enchanted young Veresai. From an early age, he decided that he wanted to become a wandering minstrel and follow in the footsteps of his father and others who passed through the village. It would be a difficult ambition to realize because although he practiced diligently and honed his skills, Veresai did not seem proficient enough to make a living from music.

At fifteen, he was sent to live in a nearby village to be an apprentice to a kobzar, but the experiment lasted for only a brief time. Because he was blind he had few career opportunities in the remote Ukrainian countryside and music was his best chance at a better life. For the next four years he remained at home, where he worked on his poetry and practiced the bandura.

A second apprenticeship under Yefym Andriyshevsky, a nearby kobzar, proved more successful. For the next few months, the teenager learned much from the mentor and over time began to demonstrate the skills of a true musician. When his teacher passed away, Veresai went to study under Semen Koshoviy in a nearby village, but spent less than a year with a teacher he found to be strict and unfair. From this point on, Veresai decided to strike out on his own.

AlthoughVeresai had spent a total of only nine months under the tutelage of a genuine kobzar instead of the usual three years, he was a keen student and the burning desire to be a musician overcame all shortcomings. Veresai struggled for years and remained a simple village entertainer without any hope of a further career until the painter Lev Zhemchuzhnikov befriended him.

Zhemchuzhnikov, on a sabbatical from Russia, stayed in the Ukraine for three years and often frequented the estate in the region where Veresai lived. The struggling kobzar and the famous artist developed a mutual respect for one another. Veresai was brought to the grand opening of an institute, where he was able to display his considerable skills and impressed many in attendance, including Mykola Lysenko.

Mykola Lysenko was a Ukrainian composer, pianist, conductor and, most importantly, an ethnomusicologist. An outspoken critic of the government, Lysenko studied a variety of subjects before settling on a musical career. He stressed the importance of collecting, developing and creating authentic Ukrainian music. Because of this he championed the kobzars, including Veresai.

Lysenko transcribed all of the songs Veresai played and later utilized them in his operas. Like Brahms and Bela Bartok, Lysenko understood the significance and power of ethnic music. He was a staunch patriot who called for a Ukrainian musical institution and who eventually raised funds to establish a national school.

In 1873–74, the ethnomusicologist published the works of Veresai, which continue to be studied to this day. Two papers would result from Veresai's performance at the opening of the Pavlo Galagan Collegium. The first claimed he was the last of the great Ukrainian kobzars while the other, written by Lysenko, dealt with the content, beauty and scope of his songs. Later, Lysenko named his only son after the kobzar. Veresai would never have reached the fame he enjoyed without this one key performance.

That day Veresai performed two of his greatest epics, "The Escape of the Three Brothers from Oziv from Turkish Captivity," and "About Fadir the One Without Kin." He also entertained the 100 or so guests, lecturers, scholars, and professors with a humorous number, "Shchyhol," and "Kozachok," a dance melody. The range and depth of his material astonished the audience and opened doors for future performances.

In 1874, he performed at an archaeological conference in Kyiv, where a French journalist witnessed his hypnotic performance and spread the word through France. That same concert spurred an English writer to devote an entire piece to Veresai, promoting his name in yet another European country. In 1875, Veresai entertained at a Russian Geographical Society convention as well as at a painters' guild, which included some of the country's nobility.

In 1881, and again in 1882, Ostap traveled to Kyiv, where folklorist K. Ukhach-Oxorovych made a complete recording of his repertoire. Despite being old enough to retire, Veresai continued to play the bandura and compose intricate pieces as a heralded kobzar. In April 1899, the great itinerant musician who was known in many corners of the globe passed away.

Ostap Veresai was a Ukrainian musical treasure. He was the most prominent kobzar of his generation and arguably the best the country ever produced. He is one of the most celebrated of all Ukrainian musicians and continues to have an impact more than a century after his death.

Veresai had the voice of a nightingale. He could sing dumy, epic poems delivered in song, in convincing fashion, as well as entertain with his humorous pieces. His powers of concentration were so intense that he seemed lost in another world. The magical quality of his voice took listeners to the many epic scenes described to them in such vivid detail.

Veresai was a master of the bandura. He understood the complexities of the instrument, which enabled him to extract every possible sound. Eyewitness reports claimed that he was one with the instrument. In a time before musicians had any special status because of their skills, Veresai was esteemed amongst kobzars.

He often accompanied his skilled playing with foot-tapping rhythms, especially on danceable numbers. He had impeccable timing and was able to deliver an entire concert by himself. Veresai's playing made the audience want to get up and dance, no matter how formal the occasion. Veresai retained the dance nuances of his native country so attached to the folk style.

Although there was a versatility to his repertoire, his specialty was the duma, a sung epic poem with a pedigree reaching back to the sixteenth century. The subject matter concerned historical events, usually military, boasting of glorious victories. There was also a religious element that told of the struggle of the common people and the atrocities of war.

A duma was difficult to compose because of its length and heavy subject matter. A testament to his skill, Veresai eventually was credited with eight of them. The list includes "Storm on the Black Sea," "The Recruitment of the Kozak," "The Escape of the Three Brothers from Oziv," "The Poor Widow and Her Three Sons," "The Hawk and the Hawklette," "Fedir the One Without Kin," "The Captive's Lament, Son of a Widow," and "Ivan Konovchenko."

Veresai had an impact upon others in different ways. He opened doors for various kobzars such as Opanas Slastion. He inspired the creation of the genre known as Dumky, a more concise version of the duma which influenced a number of Russian composers including Antonín Dvořák, Peter Tchaikovsky, Modest Mussorgsky, Leoš Janáček, Bohuslav Martinu, Mykola Lysenko, Vasyl Barvinsky, Mily Balakirev, Maria Zawadsky, Vladislav Zaremba, and Sylvia Zaremba.

Sadly, in 1876, Czar Alexander II of Russia imposed the ems ukaz, which banned the publication of books in the Ukrainian language. The ban included the performance of vocal works like the music of Veresai. However, despite this suppression, Veresai's music continued to influence others and does so to this day.

Ostap Veresai was the last of the great kobzars. The poet/musician was an artist of incredible potential who only blossomed at a later age. But he forged ahead with a career that earned him the sobriquet the Ukrainian minstrel.

Francis J. Child (1825–1896)
The Collector

The history of folk music hinges on two groups, the musicians and the non-musicians. Although the former get the glory, in many cases if it had not been for the latter, the precious ethnic sounds of many countries would have been lost. One of the most important assemblers of old folk tunes was Francis J. Child.

Child was born on February 1, 1825, in Boston, Massachusetts. The son of a sail maker, he grew up poor, attending public schools. Despite his circumstances he received a solid education. A post-secondary career seemed unattainable until a generous donor paid his tuition to Harvard. At the prestigious university, Child made the most of his opportunity. Because of his keen intelligence, he was elected class orator by his respectful peers.

In 1946, he graduated with top honors and an offer to teach mathematics, history and political economy at Harvard, which he accepted. Always the creative spirit, Child published *Four Old Plays,* and dedicated it to one Jonathan I. Bowditch, a wealthy individual who loaned Child the money to make his first trip abroad to collect folk tunes.

From 1849 to 1851, Child took a sabbatical from Harvard in order to travel to Europe, where he studied English drama and Germanic philology. He lived in Berlin as well as Gottingen for the next couple of years before returning to his position at the university. The journey had been one of personal and intellectual growth.

For the next 25 years he would enjoy tenure at Harvard. In 1851, he was appointed the Boylston Professor of Rhetoric and Oratory. With a secure financial situation, he was able to indulge in his hobby of folksong collection. Child's interest in musicology spurred him to accumulate ballad books from around the world, which he began to organize in a serious, intellectual fashion.

But Child was not an ordinary collector. A scholar who was fluent in six languages, he corresponded with other folk music enthusiasts and was able to assemble a work that reflected a truly international flavor. Eventually, the Harvard library would boast one of the finest and largest reservoirs of folklore in the world.

In 1853, Child published the first book in a series which would number

150 volumes, *British Poets*. In 1855, for example, he published several volumes of Edmund Spenser's poetry. In 1863, a year after delivering a paper entitled "Observations on the Language of Chaucer and Gower," it appeared in print.

Although the aforementioned efforts were considered among his most accomplished endeavors, from a musical standpoint the five-volume *English and Scottish Popular Ballads* was the most important. These were published from 1884 to 1898. While Child was not the first to collect folksongs, his attention to themes and words set his work apart from that of others.

Child's endeavors did not go unnoticed. There were many around the world who appreciated his sincere efforts at preserving history for future generations. Despite his scholarly abilities, he never completed a doctorate. However, he was awarded three of them. In 1854, the University of Gottingen honored him. In 1884, Harvard granted him an L.L.D. Three years later, Columbia bestowed an L.H.D. on Child, acknowledging his devotion to the art of folksong collecting.

In 1860, a year before the Civil War broke out, Child was married; the couple would raise three daughters and a son. All would be schooled in the folksong traditions. He used his love of folklore in the Union war effort. Unable to enlist, the staunch patriot instead wrote articles and ballads in support of the Northern cause.

A well-respected man, he suffered from gout and rheumatoid arthritis, but his health didn't deter him from his work. He inspired musicologists in the United States as well as around the world. His reference works, *English and Scottish Popular Ballads,* were translated into dozens of different languages and enjoyed widespread popularity. They are to be found on the shelves of public, university and college libraries all over the globe.

In 1893, Child was involved in a carriage accident which marked the beginning of the end. At the time of his death on September 11, 1896, he was in the process of completing his last volume of work. No one was capable of finishing his work so the edition was left incomplete.

Child was a groundbreaking folklore collector. Without his industrious efforts a great number of important songs would have been lost forever. An intelligent man who made the most of the enormous talents and abilities he possessed, he served as a model for all future musicologists. His diligence, keen perception, and vast knowledge separated him from others in the field.

Child brought a scholarly approach to his work. Because of this, years after they were first published, the volumes of *English and Scottish Popular Ballads* remain as the standard against which all others are measured. The precise details, in-depth research, and global scope placed this effort above the others. There was a breadth to the work often lacking in the writing of other ethnomusicologists.

Child's work appealed to a variety of people including ballad scholars, hobbyists and musicians. The high standard of his work is one of the reasons why it continues to be relevant today. The five-volume comprehensive guide is one of the strongest reference tools ever assembled in the folk music spectrum and retains a strong international reputation.

The 305 ballads represent a variety of traditional songs. In his approach Child focused on the history of the words and themes rather than solely on the music, which gave the volumes a much different perspective. He also investigated and collected songs and stories from various nations, putting to good use his multi-lingual abilities.

Child demonstrated the deep rich history in the folk ballads of America, which he traced back to their roots in England, Scotland and Ireland. This thorough research separated his five volumes from other efforts. He demonstrated an intelligence and inspiration that was rarely matched.

Some of the songs in his five volumes include "Blow, Ye Winds, Blow," "The Willow Tree," "The Two Sisters," "The Murdered Brothers," "The Cruel Mother," "The Bird Song," "The Rolling of the Stones" (a variant of "The Two Brothers"), "Lord Thomas and Fair Ellinor," "Lord Lovel," "The Unquiet Grave," "Lord Thomas of Winesberry," "The Knight and the Shepherd's Daughter," "Robin Hood and Guy of Gisborne," "Little Sir Hugh," "The Death of Queen Jane," "The Bonnie Earl o' Moray," "The Gypsy Laddie," "Derwentwater's Farewell Geordie," "Bonnie George Campbell," "The Broom of Cowdenknowes," "House Carpenter," "The Gaberlunzie Man," "The Coasts of High Barbary," "The Mermaid," and "The Trooper and the Maid." Hundreds of artists have recorded, played and learned these songs; for some they were the foundation of their repertoires. Teachers also utilized them for classroom instruction.

Francis J. Child is one of the most important historical figures in the annals of folk music. More than 100 years after his death, he continues to influence both scholarly and lay circles. The collector earned his well-deserved reputation as a man who understood the true nature of folk music.

Cecil Sharp (1859–1924)
Folklore Revivalist

The eighteenth century saw an interest in preserving the great folk music of the Western world. Many countries would boast at least one major collector, whose enthusiasm for history was a prime ingredient in their endeavors.

In the late nineteenth and early twentieth century, England experienced a renewed interest in its musical heritage. The driving force behind this was folklore revivalist Cecil Sharp.

Sharp was born on November 22, 1859, at Denmark Hill, London, into a family that adored music. His father was a merchant who had varied interests including traditional music and his mother also shared a love of English folksongs. Sharp attended the University of Cambridge where he indulged in sports — particularly rowing — and left upon graduation in 1882.

Now that his education was complete, he needed to find work and decided to relocate to Australia, which offered opportunities for an ambitious young man with his particular skills and sense of adventure. He married before leaving England. Once in his new home, he secured a position in a financial institution. From 1883 to 1889, Sharp remained in Australia as a banker, but his heart truly belonged to music.

He maintained a deep interest in folksongs throughout his rise through the corporate world. When Sharp accepted a position as assistant organist at the local cathedral, the job seemed to suit him. His previous experience in England as conductor of the government house choral society and the cathedral choral society served him well. In 1889, Sharp became conductor of the Adelaide Philharmonic, and, in a partnership with I.G. Reimann, became joint director of the Adelaide School of Music.

He became a successful lecturer. When the partnership dissolved a couple of years later, Sharp was asked to carry on but decided to return to England. In his absence, Reimann continued to build the school and it eventually became known as the Elder Conservatorium of Music. During his years in Australia, Sharp wrote one light opera, *Sylvia and the Jonquil.* He also tried his hand at composing nursery rhymes, which were performed by the choral society.

In 1892, he returned to England, which turned out to be important in his developing career. Sharp taught and composed music and much of what he taught was ethnic tunes from Germany. Eventually, the scholar became interested in the traditional music of England. From this point, Sharp would dedicate his life to reviving English folklore.

His research extended to dance and he helped to revive Morris dancing, a tradition that he dearly loved. Later, when the organizer of a girls' club in London began using his unpublished notations, Sharp realized that he needed to organize and publish his work. In 1907, he published the *Morris Books.*

Between 1911 and 1913, his interest in the lost art of folk dancing — which of course utilized the music — led him to publish a three-volume work, *The Sword Dances of Northern England.* It described and helped revive the rapper sword dance of Northumbria and long sword dance that had its origins in Yorkshire. These regions and other parts of the British Isles found a new enthusiasm for folk dancing.

Sharp had a shrewd sense of timing. As state-sponsored, mass public schooling was taking root, he published songbooks whose prime use was for teachers and the growing student population. The volumes, complete with piano arrangements, became an integral part of the curriculum and enabled millions of schoolchildren to discover their English heritage. Traditional singers from all over England also found the works useful.

Sharp reorganized many of the folksongs he had heard and in many instances cleaned up their content. He censored the erotic and violent parts to preserve the tender sensibilities of the schoolchildren. However, in his field book, he included the original lyrics with an eye to preserving them for posterity. Although Sharp would later undergo some criticism for the manner in which he rearranged some of the English folksongs, on balance he was considered to have handled the material well.

The nationalistic fervor that swept England had a direct relationship with Sharp's work. He wanted schoolchildren to understand and appreciate their heritage. Much English work had been neglected, but Sharp re-energized the genre and inspired others to take up the cause, which many did. Soon, forgotten British composers were returned to the position of respect they deserved because of the revivalist's efforts.

In 1911, Sharp took on a new challenge when he founded the English Folk Dance Society to promote the traditional dances of the country. His enthusiasm was broadcast through workshops that were held across the nation. In 1932, the organization he formed merged with the Folk Song Society to become the English Folk Dance and Song Society (FDSS).

From 1916 to 1918, Sharp visited the United States, where he continued to lecture and write about folk music. He and his faithful companion, Maud Karpeles, roamed the southern Appalachian Mountains, collecting hundreds of folksongs that were much different than those he had discovered in England. While he was there, he founded the Country Dance and Song Society that continues to this day.

Sharp returned to England and for the next few years the collector amassed his findings and arranged them. He worked meticulously, which many would discover long after his passing. He continued to lecture and collect folksongs until his death on June 23, 1924.

Cecil Sharp was a supreme folklorist. Although he was criticized by some detractors, without his efforts much of the traditional folksong of England would have been lost forever. His dedication in preserving these tunes makes him an important figure in the history of the genre. His determination was part love and part duty.

Sharp's legacy was preserved by his partner Maud Karpeles, who survived him by decades. She dedicated the remainder of her life to converting the collected manuscript materials into massive, yet well-organized volumes.

There were five such books including *Cecil Sharp's Collection of English Folk Songs*; *English Folk Songs from the Southern Appalachians*; *English Folk Songs, Collected and Arranged with Pianoforte Accompaniment by Cecil J. Sharp*; *English Folk Song: Some Conclusions*; and *Cecil Sharp*.

Sharp's legacy as collector and promoter of folksongs and dances continued through the work of others. He influenced a number of English art composers including Ralph Vaughan Williams, Gustav Holst and George Butterworth. All three had a hand in continuing Cecil's work as they passed his heritage to a new generation.

The English Folk and Dance Society, situated in London at the Cecil Sharp House, remains dedicated to the preservation of folksong and dance. Despite his critics, the old master had a profound influence on the musical spirit of Great Britain, as well as its nationalistic attitude. He had revived English folk tunes at a time when there was very little interest in preserving them.

Not only was Sharp an important figure in English folk preservation, but he was also instrumental in American folklore. He spent nearly a year in the United States over three separate trips and collected nearly 1,700 tunes during these sojourns. His recording of Appalachian songs was a vital effort because it predated the efforts of the Library of Congress, paving the way for the Lomax and Seeger families. His efforts also alerted the rest of the musical world to the rich cultural heritage of the music of the region.

Sharp established the blueprint for the term musicologist. There are two equal parts to preserving the rich history of folk music. The first is to interpret the music vocally and instrumentally, reaching out to people to instill in them a love for the beauty of the tunes passed down orally from one generation to another. The other way is to transcribe and collect the songs for future generations to enjoy.

Sharp sparked the first revival of English folk music from 1900 to 1918, until the end of World War I. He would begin a cycle of such renaissances over the years and spark similar revivals in the United States as well as other centers around the globe.

Cecil Sharp's dedication to folk music was immeasurable. His ability, determination and effort to maintain the music and keep it alive for future generations is noteworthy. He revived the spirit of the style in his home country and abroad to truly earn the title of folklore revivalist.

DISCOGRAPHY:

As I Cycled Out on a May Morning, Talking Elephant 057.

PART TWO

American Pioneers

Long before explorers "discovered" the North American continent, the native bands who had traveled across the Bering Strait to establish a society in the uncharted land developed a unique brand of folk music. They preserved their style through intense, rhythmic, textured dances which were passed on to succeeding generations. It was a great honor to learn these tribal customs which celebrated every facet of their existence, including birth, rites of passage, marriage, victory, war, and death.

Special instruments were designed to create this spiritual music such as the tom-tom drum, as well as rattles made of animal skin and bones. Dance was a crucial element as they communicated with their gods. Despite the near destruction of Native American civilization, the music has survived in various forms and today it remains vibrant through the efforts of preservers.

When the pioneers arrived in the New World they brought with them their English, Irish, and Scottish songs, which had been passed down from one generation to the next. While music was important to them, carving out an existence in the wilderness took up much of their time. Decades would elapse before a folk music tradition could be established.

Because it was a multicultural migration, each group of immigrants brought with them their own kind of folk music complete with instruments, dance, song and melody. While some folk music remained regional, some evolved into major styles including Appalachian, Negro spiritual, Mexican-influenced cowboy, and Creole.

By the nineteenth century, a folk style emerged that reflected a genuine American content. While Frances Scott Key wrote what would later become the country's national anthem, it was Stephen Foster who became the first American to earn a living from song writing, as the nation took to heart his easy lyrics and memorable harmonies which spotlighted the southern regions.

The acoustic-based music was part of perpetuating the American myth of the cowboy, railroad workers, and figures embedded in the national psyche, especially out West. Although these songs began as regional hits they spread throughout the country because everyone could hum their tunes while at work. They were part of everyday life and were taught to schoolchildren, who in turn taught the songs to their offspring.

In 1927, when record executives scoured the Virginias, Kentucky, Tennessee, the Carolinas and other Southern points, they "discovered" the musical tradition that had existed for centuries. While some of the artists they recorded established the new genre of country music, like the Carter Family and Jimmie Rodgers, others remained in the folk fold, such as Bascom Lamar Lunsford, Buell Kazee, Libby Cotten, Aunt Molly Jackson, and Dock Boggs.

Negro spirituals were also a rich vein of American music that would develop into the blues and provide a foundation for jazz, rock and roll, soul, and R&B. Acoustic-based, spirituals featured the guitar as the main instrument, but included mandolin, banjo, harmonica and other homemade instruments. Ultimately, the spiritual style would merge with the general folk genre.

Jug bands promoted some of the best folk-blues. There was a tough, sinewy sound to the music which emerged from the southern plantations and could be heard at house parties, fish fries, juke joints, along the railroads and down dusty roads under the moonlight. Although jug band-style blues thrived in the late nineteenth century and early twentieth century, the amplified Chicago blues sound would relegate acoustic blues to the background. However, practitioners of traditional acoustic blues remain active.

Folk-blues encompassed many styles throughout the country. These include Delta, Piedmont, Atlanta, Memphis, Texas, ragtime and songster blues, each with its local star. Some of the major names include Leadbelly, Sonny Terry & Brownie McGhee, Blind Boy Fuller, Blind Blake, Charlie Patton, Son House, Robert Johnson, Blind Lemon Jefferson, Mississippi John Hurt, Mississippi Fred McDowell, Josh White, Jesse Fuller, and Spider John Koerner.

American folk pioneers came almost exclusively from the Appalachian tradition and the blues tradition of the deep South. While some were busy performing, others were preserving the rich history of this national sound. Many musicians who were central to the tradition were obscure amateurs who never recorded.

Those included in this section are a fair representation of the rich vein of the American folk tradition. They are the individuals who established a foundation for those who would follow.

Arguably, Stephen Foster wrote more popular songs that have withstood the test of time than any other American songwriter.

Bascom Lamar Lunsford was a genuine American folk icon who promoted the music he loved with a passion rarely matched.

John A. Lomax was an important collector of music and without his tireless efforts many of the most cherished tunes in the American catalog would have been lost.

Charles Seeger was a musicologist long before the term was invented and is the patriarch of the first family of American folk music.

Aunt Molly Jackson was a stubborn Kentucky woman who spent her entire career promoting Appalachian folk music.

Helen Flanders was an avid collector of folk music from the New England region.

John Jacob Niles would become known as the "dean of the American ballad" for his dedication to that style.

Elizabeth Cotten was a marvelous guitar picker, who despite a late start, made a huge impact on others.

Clarence Ashley and Dock Boggs, who hailed from Kentucky, each had two phases to their careers.

Buell Kazee was a lonesome balladeer and an important link to the past music of the Kentucky foothills.

Ruth Crawford Seeger was a talented composer who discovered folk music and was the matriarch of the famous Seeger clan.

Stephen Foster (1826–1864)
Father of American Folk Music

For the United States to achieve a true folk music identity, all of the various types of music — Appalachian, spiritual, Cajun, and cowboy — had to blend. Someone with imagination, flair, and original material derived from the national culture did just that. His name was Stephen Foster.

Foster was born on July 4, 1826, in Lawrenceville, now a part of Pittsburgh, Pennsylvania. Like many of his generation, he grew up in a large family, the ninth of ten children. They lived a modest life until his father became an alcoholic. After that, the Foster fortunes turned sour and, like his siblings, Stephen Foster was forced to make his own way in the world.

He turned to music for solace and found two heroes. One was Henry Kelber, a classically trained musician who owned a music store and became one of Foster's few formal instructors. The other was Dan Rice, a blackface entertainer who worked in traveling circuses. Young Foster displayed a certain amount of self-discipline as he taught himself the flute, clarinet, guitar, violin and piano. By his teens, he had decided on a musical career.

His biggest challenge as a songwriter was to make songs commercially viable. In his teens, he started to write songs and many of them were published before he turned 20. The early pieces were examples of his search to find the middle ground between the often trashy lyrics of the minstrel tradition and what was acceptable in drawing rooms. Once Foster found the perfect tone he was ready to write his greatest material.

After one month at Washington & Jefferson College, he moved to Cincinnati, Ohio, where he found work as a bookkeeper in a steamship company that one of his brothers owned. Soon after, he penned his first hit song, "Oh!, Susanna." Like every aspiring writer, he dreamed that it would be sung from one end of the country to the other and his hopes went beyond that when it became the anthem of the California Gold Rush. Gold fever spread quickly and made Foster a household name overnight.

In 1949, encouraged by the success of "Oh!, Susanna," he published *Foster's Ethiopian Melodies*, which included "Nelly Was a Lady." The Christy Minstrels took up the song and the young songwriter had two hits to his credit. Although the job at his brother's company was good steady work, Foster yearned to write heartfelt tunes for a living and moved back to Pennsylvania.

At this point in his career, Foster had learned to strike the perfect note for wide commercial appeal. In the next few years he composed the songs that cemented his fame, including "Camptown Races," "Nelly Bly," "Old Folks at Home" (better known as "Swanee River"), "My Old Kentucky Home," "Old Dog Tray," "Hard Times Come Again No More," and "Jeanie with the Light Brown Hair." The latter was written for his wife, Jane Denny McDowell.

The songs became part of the American psyche and were sung from one end of the developing country to the other. Despite the southern slant to many of the tunes, Foster was an Easterner, but he had a way of making the South come alive through his words and melodies. The gifted artist's facility for lyrics enabled even little schoolchildren to remember the tunes.

Unfortunately, during Foster's time the music industry was an unscrupulous business and he saw very little money for the songs he penned. Copyright was an uneven practice and a number of publishers printed his material and sold it for good profit without compensating him. Although he would be the first American to make a living from writing songs, it was a tenuous existence.

In 1860, he moved to New York City, but it was not a profitable decision. His wife and daughter returned to Pittsburgh, while Foster carried on alone in the Big Apple. He teamed up with George Cooper, a humorous lyricist, with an aim to appeal to music theater audiences, however the Civil War ruined the commercial market. Unfortunately, by this point in his career, most of Foster's best material was behind him.

There were further problems. The death of his parents and other financial burdens forced Foster to sell the rights to much of his song catalog for very little money. He composed close to 100 parlor songs, hymns and music hall numbers over the last few years of his life. However, with the exception of "Beautiful Dreamer," none matched the fire and imagination of his earlier work.

Foster continued to struggle to rekindle his past success, however during a fever he fell against a washbasin at the drab hotel where he was living. He was discovered hours later. He entered the hospital and died three days later on January 13, 1864. The talented songwriter was 37 years old.

Stephen Foster was an American folk music pioneer. He was the first to attempt a professional songwriting career, but failed because the industry was not properly organized and couldn't support someone of his immense talent. Despite the fact that he had written songs which had sold millions of copies, he died literally penniless.

Stephen Foster has been called the "Father of American Music," and it is a title richly deserved. He sought to unite the two worlds of the blackface minstrel and parlor music into one truly national style. Arguably, with the many great songs he penned, that goal was achieved.

He wrote a number of American classics that remain popular more than 150 years later. A short list includes "Nelly Was a Lady," "Camptown Races," "Nelly Bly," "Old Folks at Home," "My Old Kentucky Home," "Old Dog Tray," "Hard Times Come Again No More," "Jeannie with the Light Brown Hair," "Lou'siana Belle," "The Voice of By Gone Days," "Lily Ray," "Angelina Baker," and "Beautiful Dreamer."

Foster wrote more than just popular songs. He composed "The Tioga Waltz" and "Autumn Waltz," as well as polkas such as "Soiree Polka" and "Village Bells Polka." He also composed inspirational hymns for church and Sunday school, including "The Pure, the Bright, the Beautiful," "We'll Tune Our Hearts," "Tell Me of Angels, Mother," "What Shall the Harvest Be?," "Don't Be Idle," "Stand Up for the Truth," "Over the River," "While We Work for the Lord," "Choral Harp," and "The Bright Hills of Glory." He also produced an opera in conjunction with Charles Shiras called *The Invisible Prince,* which did not survive.

The imaginative, creative Foster was perhaps the greatest songwriter in the history of the United States. Diverse artists have covered his songs, ranging from folk bluesman Alvin Youngblood Hart ("Nelly Was a Lady") to Roger McGuinn of the Byrds ("Jeanie with the Light Brown Hair"). Others include gospel singer Mavis Staples ("Hard Times Come Again No More"), and John Prine ("My Old Kentucky Home").

The wealth of his material includes some controversial lyrics. The songs were written during the height of the battle over slavery. Some lyrics are regarded as racist and the debate to change the words has raged on for over a century. In Foster's defense, writers such as W.E.B. Dubois have said "Swanee River" and "Old Black Joe" were much kinder to blacks than some of the blatantly racist material which appeared at the time.

Many historians were perplexed that Foster, a lifelong Easterner, was able to connect so strongly with the South. There are several theories. Since Pittsburgh was part of the Underground Railroad, perhaps Foster was able to speak to many runaway slaves. Another plausible explanation is that the key element of sentimentality in his work struck a deep chord with Southern folk. More than people from any other region in the country, the people from the Deep South stood proudly by their homesteads and enjoyed songs which reflected that.

Although Foster has been depicted in an unfavorable light as a drunk and womanizer, after his death he was hailed in many circles as a great musical figure. His extensive catalog had long since become an integral part of the country's cultural experience and many saw him as the genuine spirit of nineteenth century America. Years later, singers such as Jenny Lind, Paul Robeson and Thomas Hampson all performed his material.

The posthumous accolades have been many. A sculpture of Foster stands near the entrance of the Carnegie Museum of Natural History. On the campus of the University of Pittsburgh sits the Stephen Foster Memorial, a building which houses the Stephen Foster Memorial Museum, the Center for American Music and two theaters, the Charity Randall Theatre and Henry Heymann Theatre, which serve as performance places for the University of Pittsburgh's Department of Theatre Arts. Next to the Stephen Foster Memorial is a sculpture of the songwriter.

In Bardstown, Kentucky, in My Old Kentucky Home State Park, a rousing show entitled *Stephen Foster—The Musical* has been performed annually for the past 50 years. There is also a statue of him next to the Federal Hill mansion which he visited. Many sources say it is the inspiration for the song "My Old Kentucky Home."

Georgia has the Stephen C. Foster State Park. In White Springs, Florida, the Stephen Foster Folk Culture Centre State Park was named in honor of the famous songwriter. Pennsylvania has Stephen Foster Lake at Mount Pisgah State Park. In Cincinnati's Almes Park overlooking the Ohio River is yet another statue of Foster.

In 1970, Foster was inducted into the Songwriters Hall of Fame. In 2005, a tribute album entitled *Beautiful Dreamer: The Songs of Stephen Foster* won a Grammy for Best Traditional Folk Album. The effort included artists John Prine, Alison Krauss, Yo-Yo Ma, Roger McGuinn, Mavis Staples, and Suzy Bogguss. It is astonishing that more than 100 years after many of the songs were originally composed they continue to have such strong commercial power.

There have been other honors. The Lawrenceville Historical Society in conjunction with the Allegheny Cemetery Historical Association hosts the annual Stephen Foster Music and Heritage Festival. Over time the event has been affectionately called the "Doo Dah Days!" and is held the first weekend in July. Musicians from all over the United States and from other countries perform there, often delving into Foster's repertoire.

Other tributes include a CD from Douglas Jimerson, a tenor singer, entitled *Stephen Foster's America*. Charles Ives, an American classical composer, quoted extensively from Foster's works in his own compositions. Movies made about Foster include *Harmony Lane, Swanee River* and *I Dream of Jeanie*. The journalist Nellie Bly took her pseudonym from the Foster song of the same name.

Foster crops up everywhere. The Silver Jews featuring David Berman mention Foster's name in their song "Tennessee." He is part of the conversation between Doc Holliday and Billy Clanton in the film *Tombstone*. In 1928, the Kentucky General Assembly officially named "My Old Kentucky Home" as the state song. In 1935, Florida named "Old Folks at Home" as the official state song. In Louisville, Kentucky, at the famed Churchill Downs racetrack, "Stephen Foster Super Saturday" is a day of thoroughbred racing and features one event for older horses.

Dozens of references to Foster's songs are sprinkled throughout the entertainment world. "Swanee River" was incorrectly identified on the TV show *The Honeymooners*. Leonard Cohen utilized "Old Black Joe" in his song "Everybody Knows," and "Uncle Ned" provided the foundation for an episode of *Seven Periods with Mr. Gormsby*. In the movie *An American Tail*, Warren T. Rat plays "Beautiful Dreamer" on a violin. In the film *Barton Fink*, the character W.P. Mayhew sings a drunken version of "Old Black Joe." In the movie *Georgia*, a version of "Hard Times Come Again No More" is performed. There is a rousing, controversial version of "Camptown Races" in the film *Blazing Saddles*.

Foghorn Leghorn, one of the most memorable cartoon characters, often sang a version of "Camptown Races." Curtis Eller, known as the Yodeling Banjoist, recorded an homage entitled "Stephen Foster" on his album *Talking Up Serpents Again*. Jerry Lee Lewis, one of the first rock and rollers, recorded a version of "Old Black Joe" and later "Beautiful Dreamer."

Whatever shortcomings he had or controversy he caused, Stephen Foster was the first great songwriter in the United States to make a living, albeit a meager one, from his compositions. His work is the foundation of the modern folk music tradition in America.

DISCOGRAPHY:

Stephen Foster Songs: Parlor & Minstrel Songs, Dance Tunes & Instrumentals, Albany 119.
Civil War Songs, Helicon 1002.

Beautiful Dreamer: The Songs of Stephen Foster, American Roots Publishing/Emergen 591594.
Stephen Foster Song Book, RCA 61253.
Favorite Songs, Allegretto 8167.

John A. Lomax (1867–1948)
The Ballad Hunter

In the realm of folk music, performers get most of the limelight because they bring the songs to the stage. However, those behind the scenes play a vital role in ensuring that the practitioners of the genre are heard and have material to play. One of the most important background figures who was instrumental in recording, preserving and promoting American folk music was known as the ballad hunter. His name was John A. Lomax.

Lomax was born on September 23, 1867, in Goodman, Mississippi. He was the son of a farmer, but while he was growing up in a rural part of Texas, the music bug bit him hard. His interest began with cowboy songs, and to while away the hours, he transcribed them. However, as a student at the University of Texas he was discouraged from continuing this practice. Luckily for all folk music enthusiasts he didn't heed the advice.

He began working at the University of Texas and settled into the world of academia, developing excellent organizational and critical skills, as well as honing his research abilities. In 1906, while pursuing his masters in literature at Harvard, his longtime hobby of transcribing cowboy songs was encouraged. This was a pivotal point in the eventual role he would play as the supreme ballad hunter across the United States and the world.

Lomax returned to his teaching position at the University of Texas, but took sabbaticals in order to pursue song collecting. He received fellowships for this hobby, which was quickly turning into a full-time job. In 1910, *Cowboy Songs and Other Frontier Ballads* was published. It focused on the evolution of American folk material with its own national identity. Although the United States wasn't considered quite on par with other countries, particularly England, Ireland and Scotland, it was a solid folk source.

At this time, much of the rich Appalachian vein had yet to be fully exposed. Despite the influence of Stephen Foster, Negro spirituals, the Creole sounds of New Orleans, the ballads of the New England states and the drifter tunes of the Great Plains remained very much regional styles. It was a full decade and a half before the record industry would open up the formidable depth of American folk music to the entire planet.

Lomax collaborated with Professor Leonidas Payne to establish the Texas branch of the American Folklore Society, an organization devoted to preserving the genre. Just when it seemed that the ballad hunter was making an impact, he was dealt a severe blow when he was fired from his teaching position at the University of Texas. However, it would prove to be a blessing in disguise.

He relocated to Chicago and found work mostly as a banker, but his dream of preserving folk music seemed to have evaporated too quickly. In 1931, he fell ill and lost his job, then a few months later his wife passed away. It was his son, John Jr., who encouraged his father to return to his academic roots on the lecture circuit.

His comeback from the depths of despair began earnestly but slowly as he regained his desire and ambition to collect folk material. When Lomax began a relationship with the Library of Congress, he rediscovered his true path in life. For the next few years, the ballad hunter would travel tens of thousands of miles, scouring the country for authentic American roots music.

In 1932, Lomax and his son Alan recorded hundreds of songs on a Library of Congress mobile recording machine. Their first important trip occurred in the South, a rich vein of "undiscovered" music. They toured Southern prisons in the belief that prisoners, because of their isolation from the outside world, would have preserved folk music unadulterated by radio or recordings. Since many of the convicts were amateur musicians, a wealth of material was recorded.

This strategy paid off handsomely when they found Huddie "Leadbelly" Ledbetter in a Louisiana prison. The middle-aged songster would be instrumental in the folk revival of the late 1950s. The Lomaxes were so impressed with him that they managed to secure his release from prison, and the singer later worked as a chauffeur for the family. They would also see to it that he recorded with a commercial label and performed at concerts.

In 1934, the collection *American Ballads and Folk Songs* was published. It drew serious critical praise and attention, as well as scrutiny of John Lomax's transcribing methods. The art of collecting songs had always been a balance between keeping the songs pure while managing to make them interesting to a modern audience.

While Lomax continued his tireless treks across the country, the world of American and international music was changing. The advent of the recording industry had created a new way for the public to hear their favorite songs and discover new singers.

Throughout the Great Depression, Lomax continued to collect folk material while working for the Library of Congress. During his time there he would serve in many capacities in the Music Division, including as the honorary curator of the Archive of American Folk Song. At this point, the ballad hunter had succeeded in recording a number of prominent American artists who would otherwise have faded into obscurity and taken with them their valued songs.

Through his involvement at the Library of Congress, Lomax would become attached to the WPA projects. In 1936, he became the advisor on folklore collecting for the Historical Records Survey and Federal Writer's Project. Lomax headed a fact-finding mission for ex-slave narratives. An associate, Benjamin A. Botkin, carried on with the work after Lomax retired.

But the years before the collector left his post at the Library of Congress were very prolific. As the advisor for the Federal Writer's Project, he came in contact with other writers including Genevieve Chandler and Ruby Pickens Tartt from Alabama. They opened doors for the Lomaxes that otherwise would have been sealed to them. As a result such obscure singers as Dock Reed, Vera Hall and Enoch Brown were recorded for posterity.

Finally, in 1940, John Lomax retired from his hectic lifestyle, but never stopped collecting folksongs. Just before leaving, he concluded one more expedition the Southern States Recording Adventure, which saw him discover a host of new, different singers. Luckily for fans and the entire American roots music program, Alan Lomax, who had accompanied his father all over the continent, took over from him.

In 1947, John Lomax published his autobiography, *Adventures of a Ballad Hunter*. Despite this, few outside the field truly understood the sacrifices he had made in the name of American music. It would take years before the collector's work would be truly appreciated, well after his passing on January 26, 1948. Sadly, he never lived to see the true impact of his efforts.

John A. Lomax was a folk music icon. He was instrumental in keeping an estimated ten thousand songs from falling into obscurity. In some ways, the ballad hunter is just as important as all of the singers/musicians he captured on tape. His contributions were numerous.

Lomax was instrumental in recording the various branches of American folk music including blues, jazz, and country. A partial list of the singers he discovered includes James "Iron Head" Baker, Moose "Clear Rock" Platt, Lightnin' Washington, K.C. Gallaway, Henry Truvillion, Huddie "Leadbelly" Ledbetter, Dock Reed, Vera Hall, and Enoch Brown. Because of his early strategy in the prisons, the musicologist was able to unearth artists languishing in jail and unable to make their music known.

Undoubtedly, the greatest singer he stumbled across was Leadbelly. The Louisiana-born singer was not only a rare folk music jewel, but became one of the prime architects of the folk revival and had a tremendous influence on a number of modern singers including Bob Dylan, Joan Baez, Tom Paxton, Woody Guthrie, Cisco Houston and Pete Seeger.

Lomax had a different approach than other collectors. He strongly believed that one of the richest veins of folk tradition was in the under-recorded black and Hispanic populations. He managed to save a vital swath of American music from obscure non-white artists.

Lomax's contribution to the preservation of folk traditions coincided with the rise of the Library of Congress. When he began his tenure there, the institution was in its infancy. It needed someone with the dedication, perseverance and heart to uncover American traditional music and he proved to be the perfect candidate.

Beyond his collecting the work of so many unknown musicians for the Library of Congress, his work with the Historical Records Survey and Federal Writers' Project put him far in advance of other collectors, combining a scholarly approach with field work.

Lomax was also responsible for utilizing new technology and techniques for field recording without electricity. At first he taped the songs of prisoners and others with a large, 300-pound device, which was rather cumbersome. The technology would improve and he and his son would benefit from smaller, more efficient equipment. That he was willing to lug the heavy equipment around is a testament to his genuine dedication.

The Texas Folklore Society was another major achievement. Within a year after its creation it had almost a hundred members, and it grew quickly. The organization published reports and proved to be a vital resource in preserving folksongs.

Although Lomax collected cowboy songs, blues, rags, jazz numbers, country songs and a host of other styles, he became famous for ballads. They were derived from a variety of sources including prisoners, the poor, the rich, talented and not-so-talented musicians, blacks, whites, Hispanics, Asians, and other cultures across the country. He gave equal treatment to all types of music.

John A. Lomax was an important contributor to the preservation of American folk music. Without his devotion and tireless energy, many of the songs enjoyed today would have vanished. Undoubtedly, he earned his title the ballad hunter.

DISCOGRAPHY:

John A. Lomax, Jr., Sings American Folk Songs, Smithsonian Folkways 3508.
The Ballad Hunter, Pts. 1 & 2, Library of Congress Aafsi-53.
The Ballad Hunter, Parts IX and X, Library of Congress Aafsi-49.

Bascom Lamar Lunsford
(1882–1973)
Minstrel of the Appalachians

There are many branches to the Appalachian folk music tree. Although one generic term is often applied, the style features different dimensions and characters. A prime figure in Appalachian music was a musician and collector, and instrumental in the preservation and revival of both folk music and dance. He was known as the minstrel of the Appalachians and his name was Bascom Lamar Lunsford.

Lunsford was born in 1882, in Mars Hill, North Carolina. Like so many of his generation, he grew up surrounded by old-time, folk, country, and blues music played at church gatherings, on the back porch, at barn raisings, at square dances and during special seasonal events. Many of his family members were amateur musicians with a wealth of talent who never had a chance to record.

Lunsford soaked up all of this music and played a fiddle he was forced to share with his brother Blackwell. Although Bascom would never become a great fiddler like Canadian Buddy MacMaster or Buell Kazee, he developed an interesting and unique sound. He performed at local gatherings, but didn't have the skill to pursue a career as a full-time musician.

Instead, he attended Rutherford College and became a teacher like his father. Although Lunsford found a job near his home, the mundane life of a public school instructor did not suit him. Instead, he used the skills he learned in college to educate the country about the richness of buck dancing and folk music.

Lunsford found work selling fruit trees and it was during this period that he built his folksong collection. In 1906, America was still mostly rural, particularly certain parts of North Carolina, and at the isolated farms on his sales routes he exchanged material with his customers. Bascom always traveled with his fiddle while at work.

In 1906, he married and realized that his income as a fruit tree salesman would not be enough to support a family. Lunsford enrolled at Trinity College and passed the bar exam to become a licensed lawyer. During this period he continued to collect folk tunes and occasionally performed at small venues in order to make a few extra dollars.

In 1909 he embarked on a career as a lawyer, but his heart remained devoted to music, primarily the Appalachian folk strain. Eventually, Lunsford became a lecturer on folklore, poetry and songs, appearing in white tie and tails while he instructed all on the virtues of his beloved style. Lunsford played the banjo at these events on numerous occasions and drew upon his ever growing collection of material.

During the First World War, he was entrusted with hunting down draft evaders, a job he held for a brief time. Once the conflict was over, Lunsford returned to his life as a lecturer and amateur musician. Finally, in 1922, he was given the chance to preserve his vast song collection, and recorded about three dozen tunes on wax cylinders.

In 1924, he cut two of the most famous songs in his repertoire, "Jesse James" and "I Wish I Was a Mole in the Ground." Although many artists would record these numbers — especially the latter — and they were released for commercial purposes, neither made him an overnight star. Arguably, the minstrel didn't record his material in order to become rich and famous, but to preserve the Appalachian folk music which he so adored.

In 1928, he recorded again for Brunswick with the specific purpose of enhancing the popularity of Appalachian style rather than his personal career. However by this time many artists were recording the same kind of folk material, as well as old-time and country music. The recording industry was established and the world was now aware of the rich music from the East Coast of the United States.

That same year, after much planning and organizing, the Mountain Dance and Folk Festival began. Lunsford was the official events coordinator, in charge of hiring and finding local musicians to dance and play at the festival. He did a remarkable job. The Mountain Dance and Folk Festival prospered and was able to drop the rhododendron "hook" the promoters originally used. Lunsford spearheaded the annual talent search for the next 35 years.

Lunsford survived the Great Depression, pursuing his many interests as a song collector, lecturer, lawyer and occasional performer. Since the economic difficulties had seriously hurt the recording industry, there was no chance of recording new material. In 1949, Lunsford finally returned to recording, cutting records for the Archive of American Folksong.

In the 1930s, he also became active in politics. A staunch Democrat, he managed the campaign of Congressman Zebulon Weaver. Later, he became a reading clerk in the North Carolina House of Representatives. Lunsford was a man of many talents, but throughout all of his endeavors, music was the constant thread.

Some music work came his way in the mid–1930s when Charles Seeger hired him as a promoter under the New Deal. Lunsford, who had a deep knowledge of every amateur, semipro and professional musician within 100 miles of his home, was able to gather performers for the project "Skyline Farms." Arguably, the highlight of Lunsford's career occurred when he performed at the White House in honor of the British king and queen during their tour.

In 1952, Lunsford's signature tune, "I Wish I Was a Mole in the Ground," was included in the *Anthology of American Folk*. This exposed his talents to a variety of listeners from across the country. He continued to conduct lectures and performances, and to organize the annual dance festival.

In the late 1950s, the American folk revival swept through the country and suddenly the music Lunsford had promoted for decades became a genuine sensation. He benefited from the new awakening, as many were interested in the man whose knowledge and experience in the genre dated back some five decades. In the next few years, Lunsford became a popular figure on the coffee house circuit.

In 1965, he suffered a stroke and it was the beginning of the end. He gave up his role as organizer of the annual Mountain Dance and Folk Festival. Lunsford continued to lecture when his health allowed, but his decline was noticeable. On September 4, 1973, he passed away.

Bascom Lamar Lunsford was a folk music broadcaster. He spent three quarters of his life promoting, preserving and collecting traditional material, specifically that from his beloved Western Appalachia. There was a determination, an energy and dedication to his efforts which in some circles made him a legend. The minstrel never made much money from his endeavors, but that was never his intention.

Lunsford had a totally unique personal singing style. He would hit the high notes with his tight, controlled voice. He was very much a western North Carolina performer, and his roots permeated his entire catalog. His parochialism kept him from national recognition.

He was also a solid musician with a catchy rhythm. His style emphasized the dynamic juxtaposition between the up-stroke and down-stroke brushing action, as he did not practice the regular clawhammer banjo technique. He played a five-string banjo, a mandolin and occasionally the fiddle, which he usually reserved for hot dance tunes.

Part of the Appalachian musical heritage consisted of songs with bawdy, often humorous, lyrics, but Lunsford, unlike many other performers, avoided the obscenity and omitted verses. A talented individual, he replaced the inappropriate words with kinder, more gentle ones. He also excluded political, labor-directed and black cultural material from his repertoire, for which he was roundly criticized.

The majority of his song list included child ballads and sanitized parlor songs. It also featured traditional rags, blues-influenced pieces, and some down-home old-timey and solid country numbers. But no matter the repertoire, there was always a strong folk element present in all of the material which he played with such zest. The enthusiasm overshadowed a genuine lack of talent and allowed him to entertain audiences.

He provided the world with a number of great songs, including "I Wish

I Was a Mole in the Ground," "Dry Bones," "In the Shadow of the Pines," "Rye Straw," "Good Old Mountain Dew," "Little Turtle Dove," "Lost John Dean," and "Goodbye Old Stepstone." Lunsford had a strong repertoire, but sadly he was so under-recorded that much of it never reached a listening audience except through his lectures and performances.

Lunsford was also instrumental in broadcasting the energy and beauty of buck dancing. It was a strong, rhythmic, lively style, which fused Scottish, Irish, African American and Cherokee steps into one cohesive genre. Throughout his native North Carolina, there were many dance competitions. Eventually, Lunsford held dances at his house on a specially installed floor he put in for the occasions.

Despite his material being non-political, Lunsford had a huge influence on the folk generation of the 1950s and 1960s. A partial list of those performers includes Bob Dylan, Joan Baez, Pete and Mike Seeger, The Kingston Trio, The Rooftop Singers, Judy Collins, Tom Paxton, Tom Rush, Ralph McTell, Phil Ochs, Dave Van Ronk, Ramblin' Jack Elliot and Doc Watson. His singular passion and sincerity fuelled these folk artists.

Like so many other folksingers, Lunsford preserved Appalachian music. This devotion was captured in the movie *The Complete Bascom Lamar Lunsford Bluegrass Story,* which provided a fair assessment of his talent and ardor. He did as much as anyone else to save the declining mountain music and lifestyle. A stubbornly positive individual, he refused to believe that his culture could ever disappear.

A constant in his life was song collecting. For nearly three quarters of a century, he was a tireless seeker of folk tunes to be preserved. His dedication was one of his most enduring qualities and is partly responsible for his fame. Lunsford understood the cultural value of the style and realized that if it was not protected it would be forgotten and lost.

Bascom Lamar Lunsford was an intriguing individual and an important American folk pioneer. Although the number of his compositions don't match the output of Stephen Foster, in his own way, the man from North Carolina made personal and important contributions to the country's music, particularly the strain he loved so dearly. In every sense, Lunsford was the minstrel of the Appalachians.

DISCOGRAPHY:

Minstrel of the Appalachians, P-Vine Japan 5221.
Ballads, Banjo Tunes and Sacred Songs of Western North Carolina, Smithsonian Folkways 40082.
Smoky Mt. Ballads, Folkways Records B000S98K00.

Charles Seeger (1886–1979)

American Musicologist

The creation and execution of folk music as well as its teaching are vital to the genre's survival in order for future generations to build upon what has already been established. In the nineteenth and twentieth centuries there began a furious effort to collect and conserve the rich vein of traditional sound. In the United States, one key figure fully understood the concept of preservation, and because of his efforts he became the premier American musicologist. His name was Charles Seeger.

Seeger was born on December 14, 1886, in Mexico City. He developed an early love of music which flourished in his teens and led to him study the subject at Harvard. In 1908, he graduated and traveled to Europe, where he found work as conductor of the Cologne Opera. This stint lasted from 1910 to 1911, and despite its brevity, it proved to be a valuable learning experience for the young man.

In 1912, he returned to the United States and settled in California, where he found work as chairman of the Department of Music at Berkeley. Seeger was way ahead of his time, teaching courses on musicology in a few basic styles. Blues, jazz, folk, country and classical were all current forms, but the first four were in their infancy, without a recording industry to strengthen their spread.

In 1919, Seeger's opposition to World War I earned him a dismissal from the university. From 1921 to 1923, because he was an important figure at the time, he found work in New York, where he lectured at the Institute of Musical Art. The school would eventually be renamed Julliard. During his time at the institution, Seeger developed into a noted composer and conductor in addition to his already strong musical credentials.

One of his students was Ruth Crawford. The teacher-student relationship became a strong attraction and blossomed into love. Although he was much older, they eventually married and settled with his son Pete from a previous marriage. Seeger continued his work as a musicologist and during this time the recording industry was born. This fuelled Seeger's lectures and enabled him to transmit his ideas better to his students.

Although they enjoyed prosperity, many interesting changes loomed on the horizon for the Seegers. The Great Depression shaped their future, as Seeger lost his job, which forced him to re-evaluate his life and place in the American music scene. Although he had made his mark in the classical field, his greatest contributions would come in the near future.

From 1931 to 1935, he worked at the New School for Social Research, and along with colleague Henry Cowell, Seeger taught the first courses in ethnomusicology, with a curriculum very much still in its infancy. During this period, he also wrote pieces as a music critic for numerous newspapers and journals, including the *Daily Worker*.

Later, in order to feed a family which included three children, with the additions of Mike and Peggy, Seeger accepted a number of positions with the federal government, beginning as a technical advisor for the Resettlement Administration. In 1935, Seeger moved to Washington, D.C., and for the next three years was immersed in the plight of the average citizen caught in the tough economic times of the Great Depression. Always a musician, Seeger embraced the rich history of folk and saw it as a tool against social injustice and inequality.

Subsequent jobs included deputy director of the Federal Musical Project from 1938 to 1941, and finally chief of the music division of the Pan-American Union for the next 12 years. During this time, he reassessed his musical outlook. He was responsible for field work, publications, and recordings. An association with unions and the downtrodden enabled Seeger to perceive his role much differently.

Together with his wife Ruth and Alan and John Lomax, he played a vital role in preserving the music of the average person in the United States. An awakened political consciousness combined with a sense of social sympathy would lead Seeger to become a major figure in the folk realm. His concern for the heritage of the music through his trained and scholarly abilities was crucial to its survival.

In 1950, he returned to teaching. He accepted a position at the Institute of Ethnomusicology at the University of California in 1960 and remained there until 1970. In 1953, he was dealt a severe personal blow when his wife, his partner, died. With the help of his children, Seeger regrouped and continued to fight for the causes associated with folk music. He was a prime figure in the revival that took place in the 1950s and 1960s.

During the 1960s, his long and deep experience enabled him to promote the study of comparative music from different cultures. He had championed this for decades because he felt that there was much to gain. In 1960, Seeger became president of the Society of Ethnomusicology, and a few years later he was the first delegate to the American Council of Learned Societies.

In 1972, he became a lecturer at Harvard and concentrated his efforts on ethnomusicology. He continued to write theoretically and philosophically about his ideas, which had been a lifelong ambition. His dedication to the study of American and international music placed him in a very prestigious circle.

On February 7, 1979, Charles Seeger was one of the most important musicologists in the United States as well as the world when he died in Bridgewater, Connecticut. His three children, Pete, Peggy and Mike, carried on his work.

Charles Seeger was an American musical guru. Although initially known as a conductor and important figure in the classical style, he became a dominant force in folk. His fight to preserve traditional music is an important chapter in his long, colorful story. There were many sides to the man who pushed for the term "musicology" to be accepted in daily life.

Seeger was a good musician himself, but was an even better preserver of history. At a time when there was a desperate need for someone to collect, edit and transcribe the American folksongs before they were lost, he accepted the job wholeheartedly. There was a passion, a drive, in his efforts which enabled him to persevere through many personal hardships and obstacles. Seeger's approach was different than that of the Lomaxes because of his scholarly credentials and intellectual point of view.

Seeger was instrumental in other ways because of the important government assignments he undertook. Although a staunch supporter of homegrown folk tunes, he developed an appreciation for the ethnic sounds of other cultures, which allowed him to enrich the roots music of his own United States. He was a valued member of any team due to his knowledge, intelligence and capabilities.

He was instrumental in developing the groundwork for folk festivals, along with the Lomaxes and others. These large musical assemblies allowed little-known performers to make an impact, instead of toiling in obscurity. He showcased American talent for the average citizen to appreciate the richness of his own culture. Seeger explored every dimension of the word "ethnomusicology," and expanded on the initial concept.

In the 1970s he continued to make contributions in various ways, including developing the melograph, a tool that enabled researchers to compare different singing styles from performers of different cultures. Others in the field widely accepted the invention and it proved to be a great advancement.

Three of the greatest legacies which Seeger left to the world were his children. The subsequent careers of Pete, Mike and Peggy allowed the Seeger name to remain prominent in folk music circles. All played a role in the boom of the 1950s and 1960s as important recording and performing artists.

Although Seeger had various partners throughout his long, distinguished career, his greatest was Ruth Crawford. It was as a couple that they discovered the immeasurable power of folk tunes and how they could be leveraged to bring about social justice and equality. The Seegers brought the style into the modern era and are directly responsible for the social changes it ignited in the late 1950s and 1960s.

Because of his important contributions to the world of folk music, his earlier career as a composer and conductor is often overlooked. For more than

20 years he devoted his talents to enhancing the status of American classical music. He was a brilliant professor who encouraged his students to expand their abilities to become great musicians and utilize their gifts for the good of all.

Charles Seeger was a vital folk pioneer of the United States, as he helped discover the roots of the music and helped it develop a strong respect among the masses. His passion, drive, scholarly approach and intellect allowed him to contribute in ways others could not. He remains one of the most effective American musicologists in the history of the genre.

Aunt Molly Jackson (1880–1960)
Pistol Packing Mama

As in other styles of music, numerous folksingers stretch across the pages of history. Because of their contributions, personality and style, they have left an undeniable impact. The figures from the Appalachian region were unique in their manners as well as their musical delivery, including the woman who preferred to be known as the "pistol packing mama" because of her penchant for riding armed to the aid of expectant mothers in the mountains. Her name was Aunt Molly Jackson.

Mary Magdalene Garland Stewart Jackson Stamos was born in 1880 in Clay County, Kentucky, into a musical family. Like hundreds of others, she discovered the joy, beauty and importance of folk music through an oral tradition. Her grandmother taught her the songs that had been part of the region's culture for decades, and little Mary proved to be an apt pupil.

At four, she wrote her first song. She picked up the banjo, dulcimer and other instruments in an effort to develop her skills. Two years later, little Mary's insulated world was destroyed when her mother died. As the oldest, she cared for her siblings, and when her father remarried, resentment against the new wife led to open conflict.

Jackson continued to perform the required chores, but developed into a rebel, which led to a well-deserved reputation as a troublemaker. This feisty attitude was a character trait which served her well throughout a long, colorful musical career. The spirited young girl would need it, because many obstacles stood between her and her lofty ambitions.

By the age of ten, she was a regular performer at family gatherings and her creativity was heartily welcomed. Three years later, she married Jim Stewart and started a family almost immediately. While two of her children died in infancy, she raised two stepchildren from his previous marriage. Later, after divorcing her first husband, she wed Bill Jackson and they had four children. The later death of a son inspired a song.

Her musical career remained dormant for years while she worked as a certified midwife at an age before most people enter college. Jackson viewed music as a pastime, as she dedicated her energies to marriage and rearing children. After marrying Jackson, she worked in a hospital for a decade before venturing out on her own delivering babies. She always had a strong inner turmoil: whether to be a musician or a caregiver.

During the 1920s, great economic change in Kentucky shifted the state from primarily an agricultural society to one dependent on employment in the mines. However, many of the mines were owned by out-of-state prospectors who had little concern for the dedicated workers, leaving the workers at the mercy of ruthless employers. In many ways, forced to buy from company stores and to send their children to company schools, the coal miners were no better off than sharecroppers after the Civil War. The the relationship between the workers and the companies was a grudging compromise, but when the Great Depression hit, average workers found themselves in deep trouble. Greedy owners rejected unions because they would have to pay higher wages. Anyone associated with the formation of such organizations quickly found themselves unemployed and labeled agitators.

When the United Mine Workers of America arrived in the region to fight for better conditions for the coal miners, they faced incredible resistance. But as the economic struggles of the Great Depression increased, many found themselves listening to the talk of unions. Aunt Molly Jackson was a champion of the unions and used music as her most formidable weapon.

Her husband was a coal miner, and when he and his brethren went on strike, she helped the workers by writing a song that crystallized their struggle. A group of writers including Theodore Dreiser, Sherwood Anderson, Lewis Mumford, and John Dos Passos heard Jackson's original composition, "Hungry Ragged Blues." They were impressed and ignited her musical career.

When the strike was over she continued to sing protest songs and fight for the rights of the downtrodden. Although the miners gained some respect for their sacrifices, the fight was far from being finished. The exposure Jackson received during the long Kentucky miners' struggles enabled her to record "Hungry Ragged Blues" as well as several other tunes for the Library of Congress.

In 1931, at the age of 51, she traveled to New York City to support the striking Harlan coal miners. The native Kentuckian strongly understood what it meant to toil in the dark, dangerous mines for little money. Jackson's staunch belief in the cause opened doors for her and she found a second home in Greenwich Village, becoming a key part of the local folk revival.

She became known as "Aunt Molly" to a circle of musicians which included Woody Guthrie, Pete Seeger, Cisco Houston, Lee Hays, Fred Hellerman, Ronnie Gilbert and Leadbelly. Jackson was a first-rate songwriter. The compositions "Hungry Ragged Blues" and "Poor Miner's Farewell" became anthems during the Great Depression. At a time when everyone struggled for survival, her decision to join the fight and use music as a tool for change was greatly applauded.

Details of Aunt Molly's marriage to Gus Stamos remain somewhat of a mystery. Some sources state that she married him in 1931 after her divorce from Jackson. Other sources cite 1924 as the date of this marriage.

Jackson became one of the most well-known of the activists and singers because she drew more attention to herself than the average protester. Amongst her peers as well as her detractors, she was recognized as someone with a powerful message and the ability to project it properly. She was also pointed out as a radical, which led to scorn in certain quarters, but she persevered and continued to fight for those who needed help.

In 1934, the Composers Collective, which included Charles Seeger, Aaron Copland, and Elie Siegmeister among others, invited the Kentucky songstress to perform at one of their meetings. After an initial period of mutual dislike, the group and Jackson combined forces to keep the spirit of American folk music alive. Jackson was the genuine article, and once she started to perform it was hard not to acknowledge her talent.

For a period, Jackson enjoyed the patronage of Mary Elizabeth Barnicle, an English professor at New York University. The Kentucky folksinger was introduced to professors, intellectuals and others in New York society. The connections enhanced her career. Despite the fact that she was rather coarse, the socially awkward Jackson knew how to work the elite crowd. One of the more important individuals in the inner circle was Alan Lomax, the famed musicologist who recorded Jackson for the Library of Congress without her knowledge. Later she would argue vehemently for compensation, but never received any.

When the relationship with Barnicle faltered, Jackson managed through other contacts to secure a deal with Columbia Records. Unfortunately, because of her blunt personality that business deal eventually also turned sour. She recorded an entire album of songs for the label that was never released. This increased her paranoia that others were stealing her music.

In the early 1940s, Jackson remained in New York and came to understand that struggle, squalor and poverty were not the sole province of the state of Kentucky. As usual, she dealt with it through song, particularly in "My Disgusted Blues," which had stinging, satirical lyrics. Eventually, Jackson traveled throughout the country singing and raising money for the cause of the miners and other union struggles.

As in Kentucky, life in New York was one of financial hardship, but she continued to raise funds for causes dear to her heart. Although Jackson spent a brief time on welfare, her musical strength enabled her to find solace. False stories about how she survived in the Big Apple — by hustling — coupled with her exaggerated self-promotion created one of the greyest periods in her life.

In New York, she spent time with her brother, Jim Garland, and sister, Sarah Ogan Gunning, also a singer and songwriter. The three traveled together but feuded often over song credits, what little money they made, and other things. It was a hard scramble, but eventually the sacrifices paid off when Jackson was finally "discovered."

One of the more positive aspects of her career during this time was her influence on Pete Seeger, son of Charles and Ruth Crawford. The young lad took to the elderly, motherly folksinger and would later cite her as having a huge impact on his development as a musician. He would go on to become an important figure in the folk revival of the 1950s and continues performing to this day.

About this time, Jackson became associated with a group of dedicated folk enthusiasts that gathered regularly at hootenannies. She, Jim Garland and Sarah Ogan Gunning shared the stage with Leadbelly, the Lomaxes, Burl Ives, Sonny Terry, Brownie McGhee and anyone else who showed up. Although accepted by the group, her rough manners soon alienated her from them at a time when authentic folk music was attracting an urban population which later exploded into the folk revival.

Jackson would not live to fully benefit from the folk revival. She died September 2, 1960, of natural causes. Her death elicited mixed emotions as supporters mourned her passing while an equal number of enemies discounted her contributions. Opinion was sharply divided.

Aunt Molly Jackson was a complex folksinger. She was talented, but not above borrowing from outside sources without acknowledgement. She was a tireless fighter for the poor, the downtrodden, and the wronged, but often her aggressiveness overshadowed her achievements. What she lacked in polish, the folksinger made up for in drive, desire and determination.

Jackson wrote about 100 authentic folksongs, many to do with the struggle of the miners, social injustice, and death. The real number of tunes that flowed from her creative spirit could never be accurately calculated because she was known to have borrowed from various sources without crediting them. She was able to blend her own compositions smoothly with those of others to create something fresh and new.

Nevertheless, Jackson gave the world a number of great songs. A partial list includes "The Birth of Robin Hood," "Ragged Hungry Blues," "Little Dove," "Ten Thousand Miles," "The Death of Harry Simms," "Dishonest Miller," "Dreadful Memories," "Hard Times in Coleman's Mine," "Hunger,"

"Ms. Candiff Turn Me Loose," "Pistol Packin' Woman," "Poor Miner's Farewell," "Roll On Buddy," and "I Am a Union Woman." While Jackson could never claim authentic authorship of each and every song and the dozens more she performed, she gave them her own treatment.

Aunt Molly Jackson delivered her music in a high-pitched Kentucky twang that was endearing, genuine and effortless. Her authenticity was charming, but also alluring. When she first started to perform in New York she underwent a transformation as a singer in order to appeal to a more urban crowd, and did this without compromising her genuine appeal.

She had a strong influence on Pete Seeger, as well as her brother Jim Garland and sister Sarah Ogan Gunning. The latter two would play at the Newport Folk Festival, a venue that was greatly suited to Jackson's particular talents. If Jackson had lived, she would have continued to fascinate many with her talent as well as repel others with her candid personality.

Aunt Molly Jackson was an authentic folksinger with the imagination of a talented storyteller. She was a fighter and a champion of certain causes and had a tough demeanor. Her ability to project different sides of her personality to further her career is legendary. Although the Kentucky singer assumed many names throughout a long, colorful, controversial reign, she is best remembered as the "pistol packing mama."

DISCOGRAPHY:

The Songs & Stories of Aunt Molly Jackson, Smithsonian Folkways 5457.
Library of Congress Recordings, Rounder 1002.

Helen Flanders (1890–1972)
The Vermont Songcatcher

Because the United States was a melting pot, every region of the country had a different style of folk music. Although the Appalachian region is often highlighted, other hot spots included the New England states. One collector dedicated her efforts to preserving the rich heritage of the Eastern seaboard and earned the title the "Vermont songcatcher." Her name was Helen Flanders.

Helen Hartness Flanders was born on May 19, 1890, in Springfield, Vermont. She enjoyed an interesting childhood which included a father who was a one-term governor of Vermont, as well as an industrialist and inventor. She was a member of the school glee club, which was her first genuine exposure to music, but her interest in the folk idiom had not yet begun.

She married Ralph Flanders, who, like her father, was an industrialist and politician. He would one day become a Republican senator from Vermont. They enjoyed a nice, prosperous life in the Green Mountain State, which included friendships with Dorothy Canfield Fisher and Robert Frost. Flanders published two small volumes of poetry and a children's play, and had the opportunity to travel to Europe, Australia and the British Isles.

In 1930, Flanders's life took a dramatic turn when she was invited to join the committee on traditions and ideals of the Vermont Commission on Country Life. Her role was to collect Vermont folksongs at a crucial time. With the advent of radio, many people were forgetting the traditional material and performers, prompting an urgent need to collect and preserve treasured tunes for posterity.

Flanders dove into the project with an abundance of passion, scouring the New England countryside for folksingers of traditional songs with a vigor rarely matched in the annals of collecting. She recorded her folk treasures on wax cylinders and aluminum and acetate discs, and finally on reel-to-reel tapes. Initially, the naive politician's wife had no true understanding of the immense task.

Because a large majority of the singers that she would discover had never recorded, she had few leads to follow. Her best tool was word of mouth, and often one singer would mention another who lived just a few miles down the road. However jealousy sometimes kept those she discovered from mentioning others.

She spearheaded an advertising campaign in schools, in newspapers throughout the five New England states, and through numerous historical societies. Flanders encountered a rich variety of people including educated individuals as well as those who lacked a formal education but were musical treasures. Often the search ended in disappointment, but there were also many triumphs.

She swept through the New England states and expanded into New York. Many of the singers she discovered were elderly, and many had diverse personalities and vocations. A good number of the singers Flanders recorded were part-time musicians and earned their livings otherwise. Among those she discovered were Eveline K. Fairbanks and George Brown. Flanders realized the wealth of folk talent throughout New England and the Empire State.

From 1930 to 1939, during the first part of her collecting career, she focused on Child ballads. Flanders would also collaborate with Alan Lomax, the famous musicologist, who was impressed with the Vermont songcatcher because of her dedication and spirit. She found time to write a regular column on ballads for several newspapers, including the *Springfield Sunday Union* and *Republican*, located in Massachusetts.

The range of material she collected included children's songs, fiddle tunes, religious hymns, nineteenth-century American popular songs, dance numbers, folk tales and stories. Each was given a balanced treatment reflecting their rich dimensions. Numerous times repertoires overlapped and provided interesting juxtapositions of different versions of the same tune. While the lyrics varied, the musical interpretation always proved to be fascinating.

Flanders spearheaded the collection, but she had some help. George Brown, his mother Alice, Philips Barry, Marguerite Olney and Elizabeth Flanders Ballard (Helen's daughter) all aided in transcribing material. But the Vermont songcatcher was the leader, the driving force behind the important historical work. With each new musical discovery she enhanced her legacy.

From 1940 to 1958, Flanders continued to amass folksongs, but devoted a lot of effort to her family, including raising three children. Yet she found time to unearth singers who provided a treasure trove of songs which would have been lost if without her industrious efforts. This second phase of Helen's collecting career had more public exposure and therefore enjoyed greater help from the community.

As the collection grew, so did the problem of storing the precious material. In the beginning, Flanders kept the work at home, but eventually she donated everything to the Middlebury College in Vermont. The collection would later be transferred to special collections and renamed the Flanders Ballad Collection. Copies would be kept at the American Folklife Center of the Library of Congress as well as at Harvard University.

In 1942, Middlebury College awarded Flanders a master of arts degree. It was a well-deserved honor and underscored the value of her work. She was a master at transcribing songs in a manner that retained their original flavor but showed their New England roots. Many of the songs described aspects of colonial life and their historical value was immeasurable.

Flanders found time to expand her role in the folk world. She became a member of the national committee of the National Folk Festival Association and was vice president of the Folksong Society of the Northeast. Her activity level was an inspiration to everyone in the field, especially women, becoming a role model for female leadership.

Throughout the 1940s and into the 1950s, Flanders continued to collect folksongs. During this period, she authored eight books on ballads. The Vermont songcatcher also penned pamphlets and newspaper and magazine articles, as well as two books of poetry. In 1958, she retired.

For the next dozen years the work gained in value as scholars and musicians studied it intensely for its historical value. Even after her passing, on May 23, 1972, in Springfield, Vermont, the collection continued to make an impact and proved to be one of the finest that any musicologist ever recorded.

Helen Flanders was a Vermont folk queen. The 30 years she dedicated to preserving the songs and championing the singers of the New England area became a labor of love. Her legacy remains intact and her work proved to be as important as any of the material she collected.

Flanders used many interesting techniques to achieve the archives she left behind. She developed a campaign, talking to hundreds of people, scouring the countryside, placing open letters in newspapers, and contacting schools so that children could act as independent agents. She was given dozens of names and never left a stone unturned in her search for authentic folk tunes.

Like Alan Lomax, she ventured down many country lanes and dirt roads following leads that rewarded her, as well as others that yielded nothing. She interviewed thousands of people, many of whom were helpful, but others who were unable to add to the research. In an age before computers, the Internet and the level of communication that exists today, hard work was her main tool, and she utilized it to the best of her advantage.

Flanders covered tens of thousands of miles and although her outreach did not extend as fair as that of the Lomaxes, she cultivated every nugget available from the New England states and New York. There was a fierceness, a sense of complete urgency in her endeavor. She was enthusiastic, professional, sociable, but above all, had the collector's supreme dedication.

Flanders was a first-rate collector, but also a lecturer, and she wrote dozens of magazine articles. She was a humble woman who praised the singers and was always aware that without their inclination to share the folk music, her collection would not exist. Flanders's ability to gain the trust of an average New Englander was legendary. Many of her subjects were backwoods, stubborn individuals who guarded their precious folk tunes and did not trust strangers.

The thoroughness of her research and organizational abilities were two assets which enabled Flanders to complete her task. When the Vermont songcatcher discovered an authentic folksinger, she interviewed the entire family and made its members feel special. Her interpersonal skills were vital to winning over the trust of many of the suspicious participants.

The numbers of the collection are staggering. In 30 years, she recorded some 500 singers, many of whom are now deceased, quite a few who died immediately after being taped. Flanders amassed a staggering catalog of over 4,500 songs. The ballads reflected a transition from the heritage of the British Isles to a solid American culture.

The ballads expressed a wide range of themes including old world history, local events, scandals, fires, natural disasters, murders, multiple births, infamous names and children's stories. There were songs of protest, and stories set on land and sea. Others came from the fertile imaginations of the musicians. Songs described slavery, snowstorms, floods, and hurricanes. The ballads also recounted the evils of alcohol and their harsh effects on families. There were hundreds of love songs, describing bitter losses and joyful unions, including old murder ballads about relationships gone wrong.

There were ballads with themes of nostalgia, heroes, and conflict between natives and European settlers. They were sung by settlers, merchants, farmers, thieves, French Americans, Native Americans, African Americans, and many European natives. The multicultural aspect of the collected work was truly astounding and is one of its best features.

The ballads represented a sweeping history of New England culture over 400 years, from the landing of the pilgrims on Plymouth Rock through the bitter struggles of the succeeding generations who carved out an existence. In the early twentieth century, lumber camps were abundant and other songs gave a glimpse of that life.

Religion was a staple which helped people weather hard times in rural Vermont and other states. The hymns Flanders collected were rich in tradition reflecting the faith of British settlers and others. They celebrated the Protestant lifestyle and its many virtues. Flanders included spirituals from every denomination, giving the collection a proper balance.

Some of the thousands of ballads include "The Loss of Mohea," "Barbara Allen," "On Springfield Mountain," "Frog Song," "The Banks of Lake Erie," "Jones' Paring Bee," "Little Harry Huston," "Bonaparte on St. Helena's Shore," "The Stratten Mountain Tragedy," "The Last Fierce Change," "Jam on Gerry's Rock," "Ain't No Grave Gonna Hold My Body Down," "In the Dense Woods," "Suffolk Miracle," "Heart's Delight," "The Bird Song," "The Banks of the Potomac," "No One to Welcome Me Home," and "Indian Sitting in His Canoe."

Helen Flanders was an incredible collector who influenced Jean Ritchie as well as Margaret MacArthur. The latter, born a generation after the Vermont songcatcher, was also an avid collector of traditional songs from the New England area. She collected for some 50 years and was a noted performer and recording artist. MacArthur did much for the folk music of the Green Mountain State.

While Flanders was not a musician, she possessed a keen ear for an authentic folksong. The collector understood and appreciated the talent of the performers and made their efforts known. Her emphasis on the artists is why interest in the work continues.

Flanders was a special individual who dedicated a good portion of her life to preserving the folksongs of the New England region, and in particular those of her home state. She worked tirelessly to provide future generations with a tremendously important historical source. Her title, the Vermont songcatcher, was richly deserved.

John Jacob Niles (1892–1980)

Dean of American Balladeers

The ballad—a poem or song that narrates a story in short stanzas and is passed down orally from one generation to the next as part of the folk culture—is one of the most enduring forms of music. As the colonies were founded, developed and blossomed, ballads would play an important role in creating the American myth, particularly that of the southwest. They became an integral part of the country's psyche and preserving their richness fell to the lot of the dean of American balladeers, John Jacob Niles.

Niles was born on April 28, 1892, in Louisville, Kentucky. As a boy, he discovered folk tunes and developed such an interest that he began to collect them at a rapid pace. He also became a musician performing the material that he held sacred. In his teens, the budding musicologist concentrated on songs from the Appalachian Mountains, a passion that would endure throughout the rest of his life.

From 1910 to 1917, he worked for the Burroughs Corporation (an adding machine company), until military duty interrupted his life. During World War I, Niles served in the U.S. Air Corps as a ferry pilot, until a crash led to his discharge. Niles qualified for government assistance and remained in France to study music at the Université de Lyon and the Schola Cantorum in Paris. The balladeer thrived on the other side of the Atlantic for a few years, but patriotism eventually won out and he returned to the United States.

In 1921, soon after his arrival back home, he finished his education at the Cincinnati Conservatory of Music. Eventually, Niles relocated to Chicago, where he sang opera for some time, then performed folk music for the Westinghouse Company Radio Network. In 1925, the blossoming folkie moved to New York and found work at the Silver Slipper Club. While in the Big Apple, he managed to publish his first folksong collection and met the talented singer Marion Kerby.

Kerby was a contralto who had a deep love of folk music. The two traveled throughout Europe and various parts of the United States performing as a duo. Their repertoire included traditional folk, blues, rag, Tin Pan Alley numbers, and even some jazz tunes. This was one of the most exciting musical periods of Niles's life, as well as a great learning experience.

After the tour, he roamed the Southwest with photographer Doris Ulmann, working as her guide and chauffeur. During this time, Niles gathered more folksongs from the southern Appalachian Mountains to add to his impressive collection. Eventually, he published some of the reams of material in a number of books including *Singing Soldiers, Songs My Mother Never Taught Me,* and *Songs of the Hill Folk.*

He became music director at the John C. Campbell School in Brasstown, North Carolina, but gave it up to travel through Kentucky. He eventually settled at Boot Hill Farm in Clark County with his wife. In 1938, he recorded his initial song collection, which included the originals "Black Is the Color of My True Love's Hair," "Go 'Way from My Window," and "I Wonder as I Wander."

In the late 1930s and early 1940s, he performed often as a solo artist and traveled throughout the country, where he delivered unforgettable folk concerts at a variety of venues including school auditoriums and churches. He played a dulcimer, lute or guitar, and sang songs delivered in a high falsetto in order to portray female characters. His shows differed from those of other touring artists, as he delivered his dire ballads with a certain conviction.

Niles continued his dual career as collector and performer. Some of his most important albums recorded during this period included *Early American Ballads and American Folk Lore.* He was a prolific writer and composed diverse original material. A good example is the oratorio "Lamentation," given its debut in 1951 in Indiana.

One of the main proponents of the great folk revival of the 1950s and 1960s, Niles thrived as a performer. He continued to compose material, and in 1970 his work "The Niles-Merton Songs" was based on the poetry of Thomas Merton. The diversity of his work was both interesting and remarkable, much different than that of others on the tour circuit.

The 1970s were good years. Niles continued to perform although he slowed down a bit due to his advanced age. More often, he lectured enthusiastically about the style which he loved so dearly. In 1975, *The Songs of John Jacob Niles* was published. He remained one of the greatest ambassadors of the style until his death on March 1, 1980, in Boot Hill, Kentucky. The folk world lost one of its most passionate collectors, spokesmen, songwriters, and performers of the American ballad.

Niles was a folk ballad expert. He dedicated his life to their promotion, preservation and popularity. He had a knack for writing, arranging and compiling songs, which inspired others to do the same. As a collector, he concentrated on the music of his native United States and the British Isles.

Since many of his songs were derived from the experiences, expressions or words of common folk, they were genuine and authentic. This theme underlined his collected work, along with the inventive, original material. Niles understood that the richness of the style existed in the accuracy of its sound, statement and sensitivity.

While he collected many songs, he also composed many, including "Go 'Way from My Window," "The Hangman," "I Wonder as I Wander,"

"Barb'ry Ellen," "Venezuela," "The Roving Gambler," and "Black Is the Color of My True Love's Hair," among others. Many were inspired from hearing others sing a line or two. Niles, ever the creative artist, could take a word or two and spin magic from it.

A number of artists have recorded his compositions. An incomplete list includes Joan Baez, Barbra Streisand, Jo Stafford, Burl Ives, Marlene Dietrich, Marion Kerby, Linda Ronstadt, Gladys Swarthout, Richard Dyer-Bennet, Peter Paul and Mary, William Parker, Maureen McGovern, Percy Faith, Kathleen Battle and Christopher Parkening, James Galway, the Brooklyn Tabernacle Choir, The Clancy Brothers, the National Philharmonic Orchestra, Mark Russo, Joe Weed, Janet Seidel, Sandi Patty, Carla Lother, the London Symphony Orchestra & Nashville Symphonic Strings, Yayu Khoe, Sally Jones, Melanie Conrad Lockett, Susanne Mentzer and Sharon Isbin, George Winston, John Raitt, Nathan Gunn, Steve Schuch and the Night Heron Consort, Arthur Fiedler and Friends, Placido Domingo, Ying Huang, Michael Bolton, Larry Dalton, John Darnall, Peggo and Paul, The Fendermen, and Jennifer Larmore.

Niles was one of the key figures in the groundwork for the folk boom of the 1950s and 1960s. When the folk music scene exploded across campuses and in coffee houses, Niles was partly responsible for the sudden awakening to the style he had advocated for nearly 50 years. His many recordings helped shape the sound of the style throughout much of the twentieth century.

He had a huge influence on the performers of the American folk music revival, including Joan Baez, Burl Ives, Tom Paxton, Phil Ochs, Pete Seeger, Peter, Paul and Mary and many others. Bob Dylan used the first line of the song "Go 'Way from My Window," to write "It Ain't Me Babe." Niles performed with many artists at the Newport Folk Festival and at coffee houses around the country. The younger generation greatly admired Niles, who was an inspiration to each performer.

Niles loved ballads and collected them from the Appalachian mountain range and other parts of the United States. He had a keen ear for the combination of words, a strong melodic note, and a good story. Throughout his travels in his native country as well as overseas, he remained a sponge for any piece of everyday life which could be turned into a ballad.

Niles was an eclectic performer, borrowing images from other styles to incorporate into his own evolving style. Whether he played in front of a large audience at the Newport Folk Festival or to a few avid fans, he produced magic. He was not afraid to experiment with his basic sound, adding falsetto, dulcimer notes or chords, or some other form of accompaniment to his vocal delivery.

Niles was a historian and visionary. The changes he witnessed during his career were incorporated in the content of his ballads. But he wrote material which looked to the future. He collected hundreds of songs to save them for posterity. He foresaw the need to preserve the American ballad because it spoke of the culture, the era and the life of the common citizen.

Being an author brought a different dimension to his artistic side. He penned a number of books including *Songs My Mother Never Taught Me, Songs of the Hill Folk, The Shape Note Study Book*, and *The Ballad Book of John Jacob Niles*. His published work was as interesting as the songs he wrote and recorded.

Niles was active longer than just about any other folk artist. From the early 1900s through the 1970s, he performed in front of small, medium and large crowds. Part Renaissance man, part traveling minstrel, Niles left an invaluable body of recordings, folksong collections, and compositions behind. His work has greatly aided in the preservation and continued vitality of folk culture in the United States. He was and remains the dean of American balladeers.

DISCOGRAPHY:

American Folk and Gambling Songs, Camden 219.
John Jacob Niles: Folk Balladeer, RCA 513.
American Folk Love Songs, Bonnie Tolliver BTR-22.
Early American Ballads, RCA Red Seal M604.
The Tradition Years: I Wonder as I Wander, Tradition 1023.
Best of John Jacob Niles, Tradition 2055.
The John Jacob Niles Collection, Gifthorse G2–10008.
My Precarious Life in the Public Domain, Rev-Ola 138.
The Tradition Years: An Evening with John Jacob Niles, Empire Musicworks 450832.
The Ballads, Essential Media Group 31101.

Elizabeth Cotten (1893–1987)

The Fingerpicker

In the twentieth century, the dominant folk instrument was the acoustic guitar. But each performer had his own distinct style and often played the same material differently. One noted figure developed her intricate abilities as a young child and continued to perform magic on the guitar well into her nineties, amazing everyone as a supreme fingerpicker. Her name was Elizabeth Cotten.

Cotten was born in 1893, in Chapel Hill, North Carolina. She discovered music at an early age and her first instrument of choice was the banjo.

Eventually she moved on to the guitar and developed a unique style, laying the instrument flat on her lap. The young girl devised an intricate finger picking method as well as a chord progression which was part Piedmont blues, part folk and jazz improvisation.

She became proficient enough to play at church picnics and other venues, impressing everyone with her unique attack. Even at an early age, Cotten displayed a command of the instrument that few could match. At a time when traditional music was not so well established, Cotten promised to become one of folk's early stylists.

However her musical ambitions were interrupted by work, motherhood, and devotion to the church. Cotten left the guitar behind for several years to raise a family, working long, hard hours. On the few occasions that she picked up the instrument, she displayed the same level of skill that she had as a child.

It wasn't until the 1940s that Cotten resumed her once-promising career. By this time she was living in the Washington, D.C., area where she worked as a nanny for Charles Seeger's brood, Pete, Peggy and Mike. The musical family quickly discovered that Cotten was more than just the average babysitter, and had incredible musical ability.

In 1957, the partnership with the Seegers led to a recording contract with Folkways. Cotten released her first collection at a time when researchers and musicologists were seeking out lost or forgotten performers. Her material dated back to the turn of the century, when, as a little girl, she had collected and written several songs. For more than 40 years, the repertoire had been turned over in her mind and had evolved into a finished, marketable product.

One of these songs, "Freight Train," was an original composition written when she was a child. It appeared on her first recording, *Folksongs and Instrumentals with Guitar.* Other songs from this collection included "Wilson Rag," "I Don't Love Nobody," "Honey Babe Your Papa Cares for You," "Run ... Run/Mama Your Son Done Gone," "Sweet Bye and Bye," "Spanish Flang Dang," and "When I Get Home." It was a breathtaking debut and opened many doors.

Her second effort, *Shake Sugaree,* enhanced her burgeoning career and reaffirmed the fact that she was a unique talent. Some of the highlights included the title song, as well as "Fox Chase," "Ontario Blues," "Til We Meet Again," "Oh, Miss Lullie Gal," "Shoot That Buffalo," Jesus Lifted Me," and "Back Dance." It was a solid collection which Mike Seeger produced and appeared on. This provided more opportunities, as well as clout in folk music circles.

While her recording career seemed to be on track, live performances came along a little more slowly. Eventually, venues began to book Cotten, as the elder statesmen of folk realized audiences were interested in what she had to say. Cotten's concerts became part music and part narrative, as she recounted stories of her childhood. In the 1960s, an historic perspective was deemed essential, when frenzied interest in the roots of American music reached an all-time fever pitch.

Because of her connection to the Seegers, Cotten was able to appear in concert with the New Lost City Ramblers, Mike Seeger's group. The two also collaborated on other occasions. Peggy Seeger was also instrumental in Cotten's rise in popularity, performing the classic "Freight Train" in Europe, when it became a major hit. This opened up a new listening audience to her music.

Despite the success, Cotten continued to work as a domestic until she was into her late seventies. Eventually she retired to concentrate on her musical career. In 1979, a third recording, *When I'm Gone,* was released. Some of the important cuts were "New Year's Eve," "Home Sweet Home," "Street Blues," "Boddie's Song," and "Praying Time Will Soon Be Over." The recording included revised versions of songs that had been previously released.

She toured extensively and delighted audiences with the historical stories and songs that were part of her repertoire. In her seventies, she played on a double bill with Taj Mahal, a walking encyclopedia of music. As a solo artist, Cotten appeared at universities, halls, and folk festivals, and was always well-received.

As part of a project sponsored by the National Endowment for the Arts, Cotten performed on television as well as in elementary schools. In 1978, at the age of 85, she entertained at Carnegie Hall, the most prestigious performance stage in the country. A few years later, upon turning 90, she embarked on another tour, opening for Mike Seeger.

In an industry which projects youth as an essential marketing tool, Cotten proved an exception to the rule. She continued to perform and record more of her brilliant American roots material until June 29, 1987, when she died at 95.

Cotten was a folk music treasure. Her career was fascinating because of its two phases. Her skill as a musician, storyteller and songwriter placed the late bloomer in a very special category. There were many sides to her musical personality, which continues to be celebrated throughout the folk universe.

Any discussion of Elizabeth Cotten begins with her unique guitar style. She was left-handed, and therefore played the guitar upside down. This required her to play bass lines with her fingers and melodies with her thumb. This style would later be dubbed "Cotten Picking." Interestingly, she had no knowledge of alternative tunings and picked out songs in standard tuning.

Because of this very personal approach to guitar playing, all the songs she wrote had a unique sound and were very hard for others to replicate. Years later, when she began the second part of her career, her style had been copied by a good number of folk musicians. Although many tried, none were ever able to exactly reproduce Cotten's picking abilities.

Cotten had an interesting voice. She had a light, folkish timber without a deep range, but the confined context complemented her guitar skills perfectly. She didn't sound like an elderly woman; her voice never betrayed her. Without seeing her, the audience would not have been able to guess her advanced age.

She provided the world with a treasure trove of songs, including "Freight Train," "Wilson Rag," "I Don't Love Nobody," "Honey Babe Your Papa Cares for You," "Run, Run/Mama Your Son Done Gone," "Sweet Bye and Bye," "Spanish Flang Dang," "When I Get Home," "Fox Chase," "Ontario Blues," "Til We Meet Again," "Oh, Miss Lullie Gal," "Shoot That Buffalo," "Jesus Lifted Me," "Back Dance," "New Year's Eve," "Home Sweet Home," "Street Blues," "Boddie's Song," and "Praying Time Will Soon Be Over." Many of these she had written or collected as a little girl. Others were written at an age when many people are retired.

But of all the songs, "Freight Train" was her most memorable. It was composed when she was 11, and the lyrics were very sophisticated for someone that age. A train that passed not far from her childhood home inspired the song. From its very beginning, the railroad was a symbol of freedom and adventure. In 1963, Peter, Paul and Mary would have a hit with a cover version.

Cotten was a major folk enthusiast, but her music covered a wide range of styles, including gospel, ragtime, and blues. She managed to meld every mode into one cohesive sound which was definitely her own. Even at an advanced age, the talented guitarist/singer could push a song across with a subtle force that was undermining, yet captivating.

Cotten was part of the folk-blues contingent which included Josh White, Mississippi John Hurt, Mississippi Fred McDowell, Brownie McGhee and Sonny Terry, among others. But Cotten's distinct guitar-picking style separated her from the rest. Undoubtedly, during the second phase of her career, Cotten added an interesting interpretation to the hybrid, folk-blues style.

Cotten made an impact on others with her exceptional guitar skills, the wealth of her material, and the magic of her voice. She influenced a range of artists, including Pete, Mike and Peggy Seeger; Taj Mahal; Bob Dylan; Phil Ochs; Joan Baez; Malvina Reynolds; Judy Collins; Chet Atkins; Matt Valentine; Peter, Paul and Mary; Jerry Garcia; Dave Van Ronk; Ramblin' Jack Eliott, and many others. A second generation now has embraced her for all the folk music gifts she possessed.

During her career, she collected a number of accolades. In 1972, she won a Burl Ives Award. In 1984, she was awarded a National Heritage Fellowship from the National Endowment for the Arts. In 1985, her album *Elizabeth Cotten Live!* won a Grammy as best ethnic or traditional folk recording. Cotten garnered much attention as a number of books and articles celebrated her accomplishments.

She was the subject of a number of videos. They include *Masters of the Country Blues: Elizabeth Cotten and Jesse Fuller; Elizabeth Cotten with Mike Seeger; Legends of Traditional Fingerstyle Guitar; Mike Seeger and Elizabeth Cotten; Jesse Fuller and Elizabeth Cotten; Me and Stella: A Film about Elizabeth Cotten; John Fahey, Elizabeth Cotten: Rare Performances and Interviews; Rainbow Quest with Pete Seeger, Judy Collins and Elizabeth Cotten; Libba Cotten, an Interview and Presentation Ceremony; Homemade American Music; Elizabeth Cotten in Concert, 1969, 1978, 1980; The Guitar of Elizabeth Cotten; The Downhome Blues;* and *Elizabeth Cotten Portrait Collection.* Each provided a different look at her multi-talented musical personality.

Elizabeth Cotten proved that age was not a factor in folk success. At a time when most people consider retirement, she was into the second phase of her musical career. She left a telling legacy as a fingerpicker.

DISCOGRAPHY:

Freight Train and Other North Carolina Folk Songs and Tunes, Folkways SF 40009.
Elizabeth Cotten Volume 2: Shake Sugaree, Folkways F-31003.
Elizabeth Cotten Volume 3: When I'm Gone, Folkways F-03537.
Elizabeth Cotten Live!, Arhoolie 1089.
Various Artists / Folk Music USA. Vol. 1, Folkways FE 4530.
Various Artists / Folk Song America, Vol. 2, Smithsonian/Folkways 00462.
Mike Seeger / Second Annual Farewell Reunion, Mercury SRMI-685.
New Lost City Ramblers/ 20th Anniversary Concert, Flying Fish FF 090.
Etta Baker / One-Dime Blues, Rounder CD 2112.
Various Artists / A Fish That's a Song, Folkways 45037.
Various Artists / Blues with a Feeling, Vanguard VCD2-77005.
Various Artists / Mean Old World: The Blues from 1940 to 1994, Smithsonian Blues Box, Smithsonian Institution Press 0003/0004.
Various Artists / Smithsonian Folkways American Roots Collection, Smithsonian Folkways 40062.
Various Artists: Close to Home: Old Time Music from Mike Seeger's Collection, Folkways 40097.
Various Artists / North Carolina Banjo Collection, Rounder 439.

Clarence Ashley (1895–1967)
The Blue Ridge Entertainer

Many of the recording artists of the 1920s and 1930s enjoyed two phases to their careers. They recorded a few singles before the Great Depression, and disappeared from the scene only to surface in the 1950s and 1960s during the folk revival. The man known as the Blue Ridge entertainer was a classic example.

Clarence Tom Ashley was born on September 29, 1895, in Bristol, Tennessee, into a musical family. At social gatherings, his grandparents sang the old ballads that their ancestors had brought with them from Ireland. As a youngster, Ashley's surname was McCurry, but his scoundrel father ran off, leaving his mother and maternal grandfather to raise him. He eventually adopted their family name, Ashley.

Young Ashley was enchanted with the itinerant musicians who boarded in his family home, spending hours listening to their exciting stories about life on the road. He fantasized about it, dreaming of the day when he could entertain audiences and drive them into a frenzy with his wild licks. His two aunts provided for his musical education by teaching him songs and how to play the banjo.

In 1913, Ashley set out to seek fame and fortune. The young musician joined a medicine show and traveled the rough roads of the Appalachian region. He performed the songs learned as a youth and others collected along the way, while the medicine man sold his cure-alls.

A year later, he married and settled in the small town of Shouns, Tennessee. Since his income as a musician was insufficient to support a family, he farmed and worked at a sawmill. Although his employment shaved time from his musical pursuits, he still found time to indulge in his hobby, if only as a part-time amateur.

He developed a reputation as a solid musician, and found plenty of work with the fiddler G.B. Grayson, the Cook Sisters, and the Greer Sisters. He formed a band with the Dell brothers, Dwight and Dewey. The trio called themselves the West Virginia Hotfoots, and they were heavily steeped in the Appalachian folk idiom, which they delivered with intense passion to enthusiastic audiences.

Ashley left the Hotfoots and formed the Blue Ridge Mountain Entertainers, with himself on guitar, Clarence Greene on fiddle, Gwen Foster on harmonica, Will Abernathy on autoharp and harmonica, and Walter David on lead guitar. With so many musicians, the group could deliver a wall of sound, and penetrated deep into audiences' souls, with stirring renditions of traditional folk tunes.

Ashley recorded with Byrd Moore and His Hot Shots, which included leader Byrd Moore on banjo and lead guitar, Ashley on guitar or banjo, and Clarence Greene on fiddle, as well as guitar. Once he was familiar with the function of a studio, the Blue Ridge entertainer was ready to record his own solo material, which he had been honing for a few years.

Ashley and Dock Walsh would form the famous Carolina Tar Heels, which consisted of Ashley on guitar and lead vocals, Walsh on banjo and vocals, and Gwen or Garley Foster on second guitar and harmonica. They recorded a number of songs for the Vocallion label, and this was arguably the best group that Ashley had ever been in. They performed on a regular basis, often as headliners with groups in which Ashley once had played.

In 1929, he was finally able to record his solo material, which included "The Coo Coo Bird" and "The House Carpenter," on the Columbia label. Ashley signed contracts with both Columbia and Victor under different names and cut songs for both until the Great Depression put a halt to his recording career. He had built up a solid collection of material, but when recording petered out, Ashley returned to medicine shows for the next ten years, before retiring.

During the 1930s and 1940s, medicine shows were a dying enterprise, but they gave Ashley an opportunity to expand his fan base. The shows took him through many different regions and in each new town he acquired a few more devoted listeners. However, the circuit was not a genuine career builder and provided very little opportunity for advancement.

To make a living, Ashley moved furniture, coal and lumber. He performed irregularly with Charlie Monroe's Kentucky Partners and with the Stanley Brothers. But throughout the war years and after, Ashley literally disappeared from the music scene. He worked part-time as an amateur but the glory days and dreams of stardom seemed as far away as his childhood ambitions.

However, in 1952, Harry Smith released his *Anthology of American Folk Singers,* which contained Ashley's "The House Carpenter" and "The Coo Coo Bird." The collection introduced him to a new audience, as many revival string bands recorded and performed these tunes. Curious folk enthusiasts investigated his other work.

In 1960, the old banjo master attended an event where he met two folk-lorists who would revive his career. Ralph Rinzler and Eugene Earle recorded the Blue Ridge entertainer and guitarist Doc Watson, whom he had brought to back him. The session proved to be instrumental in Ashley's rebirth into the entertainment industry.

In 1961, Ashley, Watson and fiddler Fred Price formed a trio and found plenty of work at northern folk festivals, coffee house circuits and clubs. One of their live shows at New York's Town Hall provided enough material for an entire album. Later, Ashley would record with Tex Isley, a guitarist who had played with him in the late 1920s. The duo toured England and were very well received.

The second phase of Ashley's career was much different than the first because of the times. In the late 1950s and 1960s, folk music was a dominant force and those who had recorded in the 1920s and 1930s were revered as true pioneers. Many of the younger performers such as Bob Dylan, Tom Paxton,

Joan Baez, Judy Collins, Phil Ochs, and Pete Seeger knew the genuine sound when they heard it.

Throughout the 1960s, Ashley enjoyed the fame that had escaped him during the first phase of his career. He made the most of the opportunities to record and tour. Unfortunately, on June 2, 1967, the one-time medicine man with the slick banjo licks passed away.

Ashley was a folk survivor. He had a delicate touch on the banjo and guitar, and a definitive, Appalachian, old-timey voice. In the 1920s, he rose to fame and was well known among rural audiences, but just when he reached for the brass ring it was taken away from him. The talented musician waited 30 years before he was finally given his due. That he was able to resurrect his career in the 1960s proved his true mettle.

Ashley was from the old-timey style of picking. He used a G-modal, "saw mill" banjo tuning, commonplace in his native region. While there have been dozens of noted banjoists from the Appalachian region, each has his own distinct musical voice. Ashley was no exception and could make the instrument soar. While adept at the guitar, during the second phase of his career, he gave it up.

Although he was a noted folksinger, Ashley also indulged in bluegrass, old-timey, country blues and medicine show tunes. He expanded the parameters of the style in order to bolster it. The variety of forms the Blue Ridge entertainer could play with relative ease only enhanced his reputation as a solid musician.

Some of the songs he made famous were original, plus he recorded those of others. A short list includes "Little Sadie," "Greenback Dollar," "Frankie Silvers," "Coo Coo Bird," "Rude and Rambling Man," "Baby All Night Long," "Drunk Man Blues," "House Carpenter," "My Sweet Farm Girl," "Short Life of Trouble," "You Are a Little Too Small," "Old John Hardy," "Corrina, Corrina," "Sadie Ray," "Three Men Went A-Huntin'," "Naomi Wise," "Haunted Road Blues," "Train Done Left Me," "Dark Holler," and "Times Ain't Like They Used to Be." No matter the source, Ashley was always able to put his personal stamp on a song to make it his own.

Ashley added a unique chapter to the annals of American folk music. He was an important link between the birth of the recording industry in the 1920s and the folk boom of the 1960s. Despite a hole in his career, he survived to make a strong impact as the genre finally achieved the recognition it deserved, much like the Blue Ridge entertainer himself.

DISCOGRAPHY:

Greenback Dollar: 1929–1933, County 3520.
Clarence Ashley and Tex Isley, Smithsonian/Folkways 702350.

Dock Boggs (1898–1971)

Primeval Hillbilly Folk

Appalachian folk music is one of the strongest representations of the American style. While some of the practitioners lean more toward a country twang, others venture into a different sound. Some of the greatest classics in the folklore canon flow from this regional repertoire. An outstanding representative of the primeval hillbilly sound is Dock Boggs.

Dock Boggs was born Moran Lee Boggs on February 7, 1898, in West Norton, Virginia. The youngest of 10 children, he was surrounded by music and learned to play the banjo by picking it like a blues guitar instead of using the traditional clawhammer technique. Since he started to work in the coal mines at 12, the opportunity to practice and hone his skills was limited.

Although he was a solid practitioner of the old-timey Appalachian mountain style, Boggs also injected his tunes with a healthy dose of blues. The part-time musician was enchanted with the songs of the African Americans working in the coal mines and on the railroads, and befriended them. A keen student of all styles, what he learned from the black singers he meshed with his own skills to create a unique personal sound.

Despite a deep love for the music which surrounded him, he had little opportunity to become a professional musician. Most artists at the time were at best part-time amateurs. Although life in the mines was hard, back-breaking, dangerous work, it provided a steady paycheck. Nevertheless, Boggs managed to maintain his musical skills by jamming at every available opportunity.

He built his repertoire on the songs collected from the African Americans he worked with, tunes handed down through his family, and those heard over the radio and from street musicians. He added original numbers including "Country Blues" and "Sugar Baby." The aforementioned songs would become folk standards after the appearance of the all-important *Anthology of American Folk Music*.

But that record would not surface until 1952. Boggs, who was married, continued to work in the mines, eking out an existence until his wife's illness forced him to find other means of support. He ran a moonshine business for a time and played at dances for whatever money was offered. It was a tough scramble, but he forged on, hoping to do more with his music.

In 1927, his patience finally paid off when representatives of the Brunswick label arrived in Norton to record authentic Appalachian music. Boggs beat out the famous A.P. Carter and moved to New York City for a spell, where he cut eight sides that included "Country Blues," "Sugar Baby," "Danville Girl," and "Pretty Polly." He would later record a few more songs for Lonesome Ace, which was a local studio. The recordings afforded the banjo master opportunities for gigs around the Kentucky area.

The Great Depression destroyed his career like it did those of many others, and Boggs was forced to give up any hope of recording new material. He continued to perform occasionally around the region during the hard economic times, but gave up his dream of becoming a fulltime musician at his wife's request. The banjoist put his instrument away and returned to the mines for better pay. He remained there until the middle 1950s.

Boggs was forgotten for almost three decades. Like others, including Clarence Ashley and Buell Kazee, and blues masters Skip James, Lonnie Johnson, Sam "Lightnin'" Hopkins, Mississippi John Hurt, Bukka White, and Mississippi John McDowell, Boggs would resurrect his career during the folk boom which began in the late 1950s. This brought a frantic race to unearth the treasured musicians of the past and reintroduce them to the world stage.

In 1963, 35 years after Boggs had cut his first records, Mike Seeger begged Boggs to resume his career. The talented banjo player with the quick licks was 65, but like others who had been forgotten, he had not lost his special touch. Despite not having played professionally for decades, Boggs could play the banjo with the power of a man half his age. His flat, Appalachian voice with its straight-ahead vocal delivery had not lost any of its edge over time. He was a genuine connection to the primitive folk of the turn of the century.

His comeback performance was at the American Folk Festival in Asheville, North Carolina. When he was introduced to the mostly young crowd, few had any idea who he was but soon made sure they would never forget him. Boggs was given the opportunity to record again and released his first album of new material in nearly 40 years, *Legendary Singer & Banjo Player.*

The 1960s folk revival was good for Boggs, who proved that he still possessed the necessary fire, imagination and passion to excite an audience. Many younger players admired him as a man who had started his career 50 years before and still had a magical touch. He made the most of the second phase of his career and was a welcomed entertainer at numerous festivals and coffeehouses.

Boggs emerged from the decade with a lot of musical miles left to travel. During the 1960s, he had recorded two more albums, *Dock Boggs, Vol. 2* and *Dock Boggs, Vol. 3.* However, on February 7, 1971, the legendary performer with the wild licks passed away. It was a day of mourning throughout the entire folk community and many attended his funeral to pay their respects.

Dock Boggs was an original. He had a talent and style that went back to a more innocent time. There was an honesty in his music that never lost its luster, even before a newer generation. The master banjoist showed a true American spirit and his abilities allowed him to enjoy two distinct career phases.

There have been dozens of important banjo players throughout the history of the instrument and Boggs ranks up there with the best. A generation or two of practitioners learned the clawhammer style of banjo playing, but Boggs was different. He employed a three-finger method that allowed him more freedom to sweep upwards and execute crisp, single-note runs in the Piedmont manner of blues guitar. These innovations separated him from traditional hillbilly pickers and were impossible to duplicate.

The Boggs sound was a unique personal form that fell between the blues fingerpicking of the Piedmont technique and that of the classic country stylists. It was not quite pure blues, but it was also removed from the traditional bluegrass sound. His would never be confused with the Earl Scruggs style. But Boggs' personal, muscular delivery possessed its own charm.

He had a plaintive voice to go along with his musical skills. His vocal approach was one practiced in the Appalachian region for centuries and was comparable to that of others like Buell Kazee and Clarence Ashley. The distinct delivery separated him from other folksingers from other areas of the country.

He was a singer-songwriter long before the term was coined. His material consisted of introspective observations about Appalachian mountain life, depicting a slice of time that could be studied and admired by future generations. His songs told stories, sometimes tragic, but always with a purpose. A classic example is the song "Pretty Polly," which tells of a love affair gone wrong and which ends in tragedy.

He gave the world a number of treasures, including "Down South Blues," "Country Blues," "Pretty Polly," "Coal Creek March," "My Old Horse Died," "Sugar Baby," "Down Home Blues," "Sammie, Where Have You Been So Long?," "Danville Girl," "New Prisoner's Song," "Hard Luck Blues," "Wild Bill Jones," "Rowan County Crew," "Oh Death," "Prodigal Son," "Mother's Advice," "Drunkard's Lone Child," "Bright Sunny South," and "Mistreated Mama Blues." His work included rags, blues pieces, old-timey numbers, straight folk and country-flavored tunes.

Boggs had an influence on a wide variety of artists. A partial list includes his nephew Johnny Hunsucker, Roscoe Holcomb, Lee Sexton, Coy Marton, I.D. Stamper, David Lindley, Chris Darrow, Solomon Feldthouse, John Vidican, Fenrus Epp (of the group Kaleidescope), The Jefferson Airplane, Paul Kanter, David Crosby, the Horse Flies, the Rhythm Rats, Mac Benford, Nimrod Workman, John Cohen, Ralph Stanley, John Hutchison, Mary McCaslin and Jim Ringer, Bob Dylan and the Band.

Dock Boggs was an original, yet he was also one of many who brought to light the rich traditions of Appalachian folksong. A traditional singer with an outstanding, personal banjo style, the master banjoist demonstrated an affinity for the music of his ancestors to become the primeval hillbilly folkie.

DISCOGRAPHY:

Dock Boggs, Vol. 2, Smithsonian Folkways 2392.
Dock Boggs, Vol. 3, Smithsonian Folkways 3903.
The Legendary Dock Boggs, Folkways 2351.
Country Blues: Complete Early Recordings (1927–1929), Revenant 6003.
Dock Boggs: His Folkways Years (1963–1968), Smithsonian Folkways 40108.
Dock Boggs: His Twelve Original Recordings, Smithsonian Folkways RF-654.

Buell Kazee (1900–1976)
Lonesome Balladeer

While all the practitioners of Appalachian music shared some similar traits in their approach, each individual boasted a distinct style. Even those who played the same instrument used different attacks. The mountain range of Kentucky produced an original, a lonesome balladeer. His name was Buell Kazee.

Kazee was born on August 29, 1900, in Burton Fork, Kentucky. The foothill town was a good place to grow up because the residents were firm believers in family and tradition. The songs that had been around for decades were passed down to young Kazee. He was a quick study and learned these ancestral tunes, concentrating harder than other children. At five, he picked up the banjo and was soon proficient enough to play at social gatherings.

The school-aged boy loved to be in the spotlight and proved that he could handle the attention. Kazee often shined at family jam sessions, keeping up with the elders in the clan who had been playing for decades. He astonished many with his ability to deliver the hot banjo licks characteristic of someone much older. The invaluable experience of these regular musical gatherings would serve Kazee well for the rest of his life.

Although he had a genuine love of music, Kazee was headed for the ministry. In his teens he studied different languages, continuing at Georgetown College. It was during this period that he began to truly appreciate the traditional sounds of his ancestors and studied singing in order to project better. Despite this formal training, he would not lose any of his authentic Kentucky substance and twang.

In 1927, he was signed to the Brunswick label in New York and recorded more than 50 songs. Although not all were pure folk tunes, he sang them not in his formally trained voice, but in the high, lonesome mountain voice of his home. In the studio, New York musicians backed him.

By this time he had developed a solid repertoire including material that ranged from religious to traditional to popular ballads. "Lady Gay," "The Sporting Bachelors," and "The Orphan Girl" were some of the songs he recorded in the New York studio. His most famous song, "On Top of Old Smoky," which he called "Little Mahee," would be extensively covered by a cross-section of artists. Despite an ever-growing popularity as a singer, he quit his musical career at the start of the Great Depression.

Kazee married and settled down as the minister for a church in Moore-head, Kentucky. He remained there for more than 20 years and rarely sang except at revival meetings. He used his knowledge of folk songs to enhance his religious music, as in "The White Pilgrim." A commercial career in music was now a distant memory.

For 20 years, Kazee concentrated on the ministry while the world of folk music passed him by. In the early 1950s, during the McCarthy era, many artists were blacklisted, but in the later part of the decade, the folk revival occurred and suddenly forgotten musicians such as Dock Boggs and Clarence Ashley were in high demand.

At the cusp of the boom, Kazee returned to his musical career with the release of *Buell Kazee Sings and Plays* on the Folkways label. Despite his record-ings in the late 1920s, including appearing on the *Anthology of American Folk Music,* his music was unknown to the listening public. But his new record, his first in 30 years, changed everything.

Kazee played at the Newport Folk Festival. Bess Lomax Hawes intro-duced the aging balladeer to an enthusiastic crowd and he did not disappoint. At a time when the public was hungry for the originators of old-timey music, Kazee answered the call with the same fire and imagination he displayed as a young man. The second phase of his career had begun.

Kazee appeared on tours with others like Dock Boggs, Clarence Ashley and Doc Watson. He revived his repertoire from the recordings he had made in the 1920s, which many musicians had discovered and covered. He appeared at festivals, coffeehouses, and other venues. He wrote four books. Three were religious, while the other explained how to play the banjo.

He made the most of the second phase of his career over 20 years. In many ways, it seemed that Kazee had not skipped a beat despite the 30 years' absence. He continued to perform to eager audiences until his death on August 31, 1976.

Kazee was a Kentucky folk music jewel, a prime example of the Appa-lachian tradition handed down through generations. Unfortunately, his career stalled when he decided to become a minister, just as it was gaining momentum. The comeback three decades later showed he had not lost any of his spirit, dexterity and passion.

Kazee was the master of the high, lonesome singing style that characterized the Appalachian balladeer. There was a sensitive quality to his sound that was a direct result of learning how to sing in the Kentucky foothill region. Although a local performer, Kazee was appreciated by a wider audience throughout the country, as well internationally. The vocalist's distinct regional tone had enough appeal to interest those outside of his home state.

Although he was a good musician, his true musical gift was in his singing style, which captivated audiences. There was a lonesome, haunting element in his ability to emote in the best Kentucky tradition. Kazee touched a nerve with his vocal delivery that few other singers could. The high-pitched voice brought to life the material he played with such expertise.

Kazee was a solid banjo player. He learned his lessons well as a youngster and improved on the tradition of his ancestors by retaining the old while adding a distinct, personal touch. There was an energy to his style which was characteristic of its Kentucky roots. Although Kazee could play with pure fire, he had a special touch which proved that he was more than just the average instrumentalist.

He was also a more than adequate pianist. However this dimension of his musical ability was never fully exposed. There are very few recordings of him on the piano, but Kazee approached it much like the banjo. The piano was not part of the Appalachian tradition, and the majority of the amateur musicians preferred banjo, fiddle and guitar.

Kazee was also a folklorist, because he kept alive the songs of his people and packaged them in such a way that they appealed to a modern audience. This was a special talent. He was able to maintain the original charm of the pieces. The ability to translate traditional American songs for modern audiences was one of his most impressive talents.

He was responsible for introducing a number of standard Appalachian numbers from the past into the contemporary fold. His repertoire consisted of a mixture of old standards and originals. A short list includes "Roll On John," "Old Whisker Bill," "The Ship That's Sailing High on the Water," "The Roving Cowboy," "The Old Maid," "Lady Gray," "The Wagoner's Lads," "Little Bessie," ""Married Girl Troubles," "Gamblin' Blues," and "Cowboy Trail." Whether he sang one of his own compositions or one which had existed for hundreds of years, each number was given special attention.

His live appearances were well received because the same sincerity and honesty found on the records was transmitted on the stage. He dressed in overalls and a checkered shirt for most events, and delighted the crowd with his banjo and occasionally the piano. What he was able to bring across were the roots of the songs he played, shedding light on the depth of their beauty.

In many ways, Kazee never received a fair amount of attention. The 52 songs he recorded in the 1920s and his later releases provided some exposure. But it was the June Appal recording in 1978 which truly exposed him to a wider audience. Sadly, this came two years after his death. The recording was a project of love that involved his family and reflects his true musical tastes. In 2007, a number of organizations including the Appalshop Archive and Berea College's Appalachian Sound Archives, and an assortment of individuals all came together to release the work, *Buell Kazee*.

He had large influence on a number of musicians. A partial list includes Doc Watson, Bob Dylan, Earl Scruggs, Dock Boggs, Clarence Ashley, John Cohen, Phil Ochs, Judy Collins, and Joan Baez. Although he was a first-rate singer and songwriter, because of his few recordings, Kazee remained a mystery to many. Only after the posthumous release did he attract the attention which had always eluded him.

Buell Kazee was one of the best representatives of the high mountain singing style that the Appalachian region ever produced. Despite a career interrupted by his work as a minister, he remains one of the best of the early folk artists. The lonesome balladeer eventually received the credit he was due.

DISCOGRAPHY:

Buell Kazee Sings and Plays, Smithsonian Folkways 3810.
Buell Kazee, June Appal JA0009.
Legendary Kentucky, British Archive of Country Music 027.

Ruth Crawford Seeger
(1901–1953)
Folk Music Matriarch

In every style of music there are people who stand out because of their longevity, creativity and contributions. There are many figures in folk that are important due to their influences in shaping the sound of others. Only a marriage can create a special musical union with broad-reaching consequences. That's what happened in the case of Ruth Crawford Seeger, a folk music matriarch.

Ruth Porter Crawford was born on July 3, 1901, in East Liverpool, Ohio.

Her childhood was one of religion, traveling and conservatism. Her father, a Methodist minister, moved his family around as he undertook different posts around the country. When Ruth was 13, her father died and left his family stranded in Jacksonville, Florida.

By this time, the young Crawford had developed a keen interest in music, as well as poetry. In a matter of only a few years she became an accomplished pianist and enrolled in the Foster School of Musical Art in Florida. However, at the age of 20, born with the same wanderlust as her father, she moved to Chicago, where greater opportunities were available.

During her teen years she had developed poetry sketches, but in the Windy City she honed her compositional skills. Crawford's musical education exposed her to opera, symphonic music and the avant-garde of the day. Her study of composition and theory under Adolf Weidig (whose father had learned from the great master Johannes Brahms) was an important step in her evolution as a songwriter.

Crawford was encouraged to create original material and further enhanced her promise when she studied piano under Djana Lavoi-Herz. He encouraged her to study music concentrating on theosophy, which opened up the world of European religions and modernism, as well as American transcendentalism. She kept company with an interesting mix of avant-garde composers including Dane Rudhyar, Aaron Copland, Carl Ruggles and Henry Cowell. The influence of these intellectuals enabled her to create sophisticated works in the mid–1920s that gained considerable attention from a variety of sources.

In 1924, she composed *Piano Preludes*, which broke new ground for women. The subsequent performances of her various compositions placed her in elite company. With each new piece, *Violin and Piano* and *Suite for Five Wind Instruments and Piano*, Crawford enhanced a blossoming reputation that had caught the attention of noted composers around the world. Interestingly, she also collaborated with poet Carl Sandburg on a number of folksong arrangements. It was her first, but not her last, foray into this style.

In 1929, she moved to New York, where she came under the guidance of Charles Seeger, a noted composer and musicologist. Although it began as a teacher-student relationship, eventually it blossomed into love. The romance was put on hold when she won a Guggenheim fellowship to study in Europe, where she met Béla Bartók, Alexander Mosolov, William Walton, Alban Berg, Paul Hindemith and Josef Rufer.

Crawford had earned a reputation for composing and the sojourn overseas proved to be a finishing school. She reached full maturity in works such as *Three Chants*, *String Quartet*, and *Three Songs*. Although the European trip was a worthwhile adventure, her love for Charles proved to be an overpowering force.

In 1931, Crawford returned from Europe and wrote *String Quartet,* considered a masterpiece of modern classical music. In 1932, she sacrificed her cherished musical career to raise a family after she married Charles Seeger. She helped raise his son Pete, from a previous marriage, and bore Peggy and Mike. All three would grow up to be influential folksingers.

The Great Depression was hard on the Seeger family, as work was scarce for Charles until he managed to find employment with a government relief agency. It enabled them to travel to many downtrodden communities. Here Ruth and her husband developed a strong social consciousness over the plight of families in isolated regions across the country. The experience would transform them from classical composers to writers, collectors and transcribers of authentic folk music.

In their new musical path, Ruth connected with the prime folk music collectors, John and Alan Lomax. In 1936, the Seegers moved to Washington, D.C., where they worked for the Library of Congress collection preserving the rich vein of American traditional music. This deep interest joined with a new political awakening brought about by the Great Depression.

This shift in political points of view and indulgence in folk music propelled them to embrace social and cultural change. Ruth Seeger wrote some of the strongest, most militant songs, including "Sacco, Vanzetti" and "Chinaman, Laundryman." The depth of their involvement in issues of social justice and equality would eventually lead them to the American Communist Party.

Although they were involved in many things, Ruth spent most of the 1940s teaching children how to play the piano. In 1948, she published *American Folk Songs for Children.* Later volumes included *Our Singing Country, Animal Folk Songs for Children,* and *American Folk Songs for Christmas.* It was a satisfying role and while she shaped young minds, Crawford also kept one foot in the political arena.

In 1950, after years of inactivity, she returned to composing to produce *Suite for Wind Quintet,* which combined her interest in modernism and folk music. Not long after completing the piece, she was diagnosed with intestinal cancer. On November 18, 1953, Ruth Crawford Seeger died in Chevy Chase, Maryland.

Ruth Crawford Seeger was a folk music beacon. Her reputation as a musician has grown and to many she remains one of the most important American female composers of the twentieth century, if not the most important. While her body of work is small, it is the quality and not the quantity that is vital. Interest in her work continues to this day after reissues of the material. A generation of American composers value her integral contributions.

Crawford was a woman of many talents. She was a first-rate composer, a capable musician, a teacher and a prime ethnomusicologist long before the term had been coined. Her range is both impressive and breathtaking because she was at the forefront of the American avant garde when few females were in the field.

But her contributions as a folk collector, teacher, and activist are of greatest interest for this book. Along with her husband Charles, Ruth Seeger was a pioneer in an ever-widening field. Her sincere passion earned her a reputation as a leader in the folk music environment.

The songs she wrote for children were instructive and made her one of the most important teachers of traditional sound. She took the tradition of one generation passing its music to another orally and turned it into material for children to be used in schools and homes. The songs were there in books for future students.

She was also a historian. Her tireless work in transcribing, arranging and editing hundreds of American folksongs helped preserve the country's rich music. Seeger could transcribe a song without losing any part of it. She ranks with the Lomaxes in helping the Library of Congress preserve the music for posterity.

She taught hundreds of children how to play the piano and appreciate the richness and beauty of folk music. Perhaps her three greatest pupils were her children, Pete, Mike and Peggy. All would make their mother proud, playing a vital role in the folk music world over the next 50 years. After she died, these lessons would be carried over to the folk boom years.

Ruth Crawford Seeger was a complex person whose contributions rival the efforts of nearly all others. She understood the power of song and used it to improve the lives of many who had fallen on hard times. She was the matriarch not only of the Seeger dynasty, but of all those in the folk music idiom.

WORKS (ON LP):

Five Songs to Poems of Carl Sandburg, songs (5) for voice & piano.
20th/21st Century Music for Voice and Keyboard (vocal).
Piano Study in Mixed Accents (for piano).
Etude for Keyboard (keyboard).
String Quartet 1931 Quartet for Four String Instruments (chamber).
Suite (for wind quintet).
Quintet for Five Woodwind Instruments (chamber).
Three Chants (for women's chorus).
Secular Choral Music (choral).

Part Three

Political Connections

For centuries, folk music concentrated on subjects like holidays (especially Christmas), ordinary people, love affairs gone wrong, monarchy (satirically handled), history, people like cowboys and railroad workers, nature, and later, national/mythical figures. There was an innocence reflected in the lyrics of these songs.

However, the industrial age changed everything. Suddenly, the plight of the average worker became a very important topic and found its way into folk music. When those who toiled in factories for little money formed unions, they used folk music as a tool for social justice and change. The connection of folk music and politics was born.

The first folksinger to directly utilize the music as leverage in negotiations for the common worker was Joe Hill. He was an outspoken political radical and set the tone for all who followed. The troubadour fought for the union cause and was always just one step ahead of the law, until it caught up to him. In the eyes of his union brethren, he became a martyr.

Changes brought about by song lyrics took on a new dimension with the advent of the Great Depression. With millions unemployed and living in makeshift camps, folk music gave rise to the protest song. Woody Guthrie led the way, fighting his entire life for the rights of the common working person. He penned many tunes and firmly established the role of the modern singer-songwriter.

Guthrie traveled from one end of the country to the other broadcasting his political views through folksongs, and along the way made friends with some kindred spirits. These included Pete Seeger, Cisco Houston, Burl Ives, Josh White, Lee Hays, Fred Hellerman, Ronnie Gilbert and Leadbelly, when that artist became more political in the later part of his career. They withstood personal threats to support the struggle for change.

The politics of the folk protest movement were left-wing and often supported Communism, clashing with democracy and the beliefs that founded the country. Because of this political stance, many of the folkies were labeled radicals, troublemakers and a threat to national security.

The price the political folk practitioners would pay would be heavy in the 1950s, during the McCarthy era and the "Red" scare. McCarthy flushed out many of the musicians, blacklisting them and keeping them from performing in theaters and concert halls and on television and radio. In the first part of the decade, folk music reached a very low ebb of popularity.

But politically-oriented folk music survived, as Guthrie paved the way for the later emergence of Bob Dylan, Phil Ochs, Arlo Guthrie, Utah Phillips, Fred Small, Dick Gaughan, Country Joe McDonald, Millard Lampell, Holly Near, Scott Alack, Alix Dobkin, Jez Lowe, Magpie, Edward Seaga, Tommy Sands, Joan Baez, Ramblin' Jack Elliott and Tom Rush, among others. During the folk revival, many political and social issues fueled the new generation of folk protesters.

Often, individuals combined their respective talents to form powerful groups. In the 1940s, the Almanac Singers carried a strong political message in their music. Later, the Weavers continued where the Almanac Singers left off. Dozens of groups formed during the folk boom.

Politically-oriented folk music would later split into various branches, including folk-rock, contemporary folk, urban folk, singer-songwriter music, and anti-folk. Political music performers have always been defiant and rebellious, their music challenging the standard doctrine of the day.

Although the United States and Great Britain have produced the greatest number of politically-oriented artists, the protest song became an international tool for change. Musicians from all over the planet plugged into the idea. Despite the dangers in nations ruled by dictators, wherever people struggle, someone has a song to aid their cause. The global fight for equality, justice and rights is supported by many folk artists.

The political connections of folk music inspire activism on a wide range of causes, from current headlines to long-term issues. The government and specific individuals have been satirized and ridiculed and turned to face their mistakes. Folk songs have targeted and supported celebrities, deviants, and special groups. Subjects of protest always abound.

Politically-inspired artists have made enormous contributions to the folk idiom and represent some of the finest musicians in the history of the style. For the past 70 years they have created their own branch of the traditional music tree.

Joe Hill was the first to write politically charged material in order to bring about change. Burl Ives was the most subtle political folk artist. He conquered all media. Earl Robinson was known as much for his political beliefs as he was his musical ability. Woody Guthrie was the most important folk musician of his day, and his protest songs inspired all future generations. Lee Hays was a fervent political folkie and one of the Almanac Singers. Josh White mixed blues and gospel with his folk tunes to bring about social change.

Cisco Houston was Woody Guthrie's traveling partner, who also enjoyed a solid career on his own.

Joe Glazer was heavily involved in labor protests and used his musical abilities to help the common working person in his fight for better conditions. Pete Seeger was a famous member of the first family of American folk and carried on admirably in his father's and stepmother's footsteps. Fred Hellerman was an integral member of the Weavers, who enjoyed a strong solo career.

Joe Hill (1879–1915)

The Initiator

The connection between folk music and politics added a new dimension to the genre. Audience perception, lyrical content and the attitude of the performers changed and as music began to be utilized as a tool for social equality and justice. The first artist who used folk music politically was Joe Hill.

Hill was born Joel Emmanuel Haggland on January 7, 1879, in Gayle, Sweden. His father, a railroad worker, died when Joe was eight. Little is known about his childhood, but somewhere he picked up an interest in music and started to hone his talents. He delved into classical music as well as the folk music of his country, a rich heritage which included a strong element of dance.

But it was very difficult to launch a musical career in Sweden, and other employment opportunities seemed limited. Hill was a restless spirit who craved new adventures and ached for release. In 1902, after his mother died, he emigrated to the United States and settled in the San Francisco Bay area. This was the first step in his transformation into a protest singer.

In 1906, he survived the San Francisco earthquake and sent a horrific account of the tragic event back to Sweden. Hill then disappeared for a few years. There is a good chance that he was drifting from one job to another, perhaps trying to make it as a musician, and wary of the law, trying to stay one step ahead at all times. He already had been in trouble with the authorities.

In 1910, he resurfaced in San Pedro, California, as a migrant laborer who had firsthand experience of the suffering migrant families endured. By this time he had changed his name to Joseph Hillstrom, and was in many ways an American, after living in the country for eight years. More importantly, he had picked up a strong political consciousness along the way, and was ready to become a social activist.

In San Pedro, he joined the International Workers of the World, a Chicago-based organization that was known as the Wobblies. The outfit's goal was to unionize industries in order to gain rights for the workers. He aligned himself with the I.W.W., declaring membership in the Portland chapter under the name Joe Hill. He performed at rallies and was considered by many to be a full-fledged folk protester. However, the authorities considered him a radical and a troublemaker, and kept an eye on his activities.

By 1911, Hill had relocated to Tijuana, Mexico, and was embroiled in a plot to overthrow the government. Because of his political activities, officials were determined to catch him, but he managed to escape their security net. For the next three years, many reported Joe Hill sightings, but many of those proved to be false.

Hill had developed his musical abilities to play at I.W.W. rallies, where he sang inflammatory songs with lyrics that harshly criticized capitalist bosses. The words to these fiery songs would be published in the union organization's *Little Red Song Books*, which were widely distributed. The immigrant from Sweden had become a genuine folk hero to the working class poor, and a bête noire in the eyes of the authorities.

Workers throughout the country already knew the lyrics to such classics as "Union Maid," "The Preacher and the Slave," "There Is a Power in the Union," and "Workers of the World, Awaken!" not from books, but from Hill's performances. Many of the songs were set to well-known folk numbers. This made his work less original, but facilitated the learning process.

For years, Joe Hill had eluded the authorities. In January 1914, he was captured in Salt Lake City, Utah, and charged under very controversial circumstances with the murder of a grocer, who was a retired police officer. The trial featured a defiant defendant who, according to witnesses, was openly hostile to the jury, the judge and his own lawyers. Justice was swift and final. Hill was executed on November 19, 1915.

Although he had some strong political figures in his corner, including President Woodrow Wilson, Hill seemed bent on becoming a martyr for the state of the common laborer. After his death, his coffin was paraded through the streets of Chicago, where thousands of mourners held a silent vigil for the man who had changed so many lives. His execution forever cemented his legend in union circles.

Joe Hill was a political songwriter. Although not original or prolific, he managed to create a catalog of 30 songs. While they were few, they were explosive. Many provoked such strong sentiments that they were rarely performed in public.

Joe Hill delivered his songs like a workingman, with only minor musical talent. He had neither a deep, rich voice nor particularly strong instrumental abilities. But there was something catchy about his songs that inspired those that sang them to rally for the union cause. In this respect, he was very effective.

He was the prime originator of the left-wing political branch of folk music, later embraced by others including Woody Guthrie, Cisco Houston, Pete Seeger, Bob Dylan, and Joan Baez. While the Red-bashing in the 1950s initially silenced the American left and forced it to go underground for the first half of the decade, Joe Hill remained a vibrant influence on those who believed in his cause.

A decade after his controversial death by firing squad, an anthem titled "Joe Hill" became part of the folk repertoire. It was written by Alfred Hayes, a poet, and put to music by Earl Robinson. In the 1930s and 1940s, it was sung at worker rallies to remind many of the sacrifices that Hill had made during his lifetime for the cause. In 1969, at the Woodstock Festival, Joan Baez delivered a haunting version as her opening number.

Others have given notable performances. Paul Robeson and Pete Seeger often incorporated the song into their repertoires. The Dubliners cut their own interpretation. Scott Walker included a version on his album *The Moviegoer*. Phil Ochs composed a variation which garnered significant attention after it was recorded. Later, Billy Bragg, one of the new political folk warriors, wrote "I Dreamed I Saw Phil Ochs Last Night," which was a reworking of the initial Hayes-Robinson original. Frank Tovey, on his album, *Tyranny and the Hired Hand*, made reference to Hill.

Bob Dylan, considered by many to be the messiah of the modern folk movement, was truly inspired by Hill's life and beliefs. At various times, he claimed that the Swedish labor activist inspired Dylan's songwriting and was the root of the song "I Dreamed I Saw St. Augustine." The most celebrated folkie of the early 1960s, Dylan would also write inflammatory songs.

The group Chumbawamba's song about Joe Hill, entitled "By and By," appeared on their album *A Singsong and a Scrap*. In 1990, the label Smithsonian Folkways released *Don't Mourn — Organize! Songs of Labor Songwriter Joe Hill*. The album featured the posthumous contributions of Cisco Houston, Haywire Mac McClintock, Utah Phillips, and Elizabeth Gurley Flynn, among others. It was a touching tribute and demonstrated that 75 years after his execution, Hill still garnered tremendous respect in the folk community.

Eventually, others from his native country made contributions. Ture Nerman, a Swedish socialist leader, wrote a biography simply titled *Joe Hill*. The book included interviews with many of Hill's family members. Nerman also translated Hill's entire song catalog into Swedish. Later the punk rock band Randy included their countryman and his organization Industrial Workers of the World in a song on their CD *The Human Atom Bombs,* released in 2001.

There have been other literary efforts. Wallace Stegner published a fictional biography titled *Joe Hill*. Gibbs M. Smith wrote *Joe Hill*, which was turned into a movie in 1971. John Dos Passos, the American novelist, dedicated a chapter to Hill in his novel *1919*. In 1999, Fred Alpi, the Swedish-French vocalist, wrote a song titled "Chanson pour Joe Hill." In 2008, composer and bandleader Wayne Horvitz wrote an orchestral work as a tribute to Hill.

Interestingly, since the recording industry didn't exist during Hill's lifetime, he never recorded any of his songs. But with the oral folk tradition, many other artists incorporated Hill's lyrical phrases and themes into their personal catalog. To many, the feeling, the spirit and the belief of Joe Hill was more captivating than the scant biographical material. The Swedish radical provided a rich foundation for future songwriters.

Joe Hill was a legend long before his untimely death. He was the first protest singer in America and set the tone for all others to follow. A controversial figure, he was, after all aspects of his life are carefully examined, an important turning point in the development of the folksong as a political tool.

Burl Ives (1909–1995)
The Wayfarin' Stranger

Folk music is rich with varied personalities who made the genre vibrant, energetic and appealing. Artists came from all over the country and had intimate life experiences that helped shape their distinct sound. One of these individuals earned a tremendous amount of popularity throughout his career as the "wayfarin' stranger." His name was Burl Ives.

Ives was born June 14, 1909, in Huntington Township, Jasper County, Illinois. From the age of four, he developed a strong interest in music that remained dominant throughout his entire life. He was a keen student at his grandmother's knee and memorized Scottish, English and Irish ballads. The burly young boy grew up with a song in his heart.

He attended Charleston Teachers College and New York University, but never became a teacher. Instead, he educated people about the beauty of folk music during his long career as an entertainer. He played pro football for a while, but gave it up to pursue his interests as a performer.

Like so many folk musicians before him, Ives hitchhiked across the country and collected the raw material for the cycle of songs which would someday make him famous. In 1937, he landed in New York City and a year later made his Broadway debut. He doubled as a folksinger in Greenwich Village clubs and built a strong local following.

In the 1940s, his tremendous gifts as a guitarist and singer enabled him to secure radio work, including his own show, *The Wayfarin' Stranger*, on CBS. On the program he performed "Lavender Blue," "Foggy, Foggy Dew," "Blue Tail Fly," and "Big Rock Candy Mountain," all derived from folk sources. In 1942/43, he served in the Army and Air Force before being honorably discharged.

Back on the air, he had other opportunities and was able to record for the first time on a small label before Decca signed him. In 1945, he married Helen Peck Ehrlich. In 1946, he made his movie debut in the film *Smoky*. In 1948, he continued to display multiple talents with the publication of his first book, *The Wayfaring Stranger*. A year later, his song "Lavender Blue (Dilly Dilly)," hit the charts, which ignited a string of top ten tunes. Already, he was a performer with many sides to his career, which ensured that he would always be employed.

About this time the long-playing (LP) record came into fashion, which was a boon for Ives. In the next few years, he would release a number of albums on the Stinson, Decca and Columbia labels. He rolled out *The Wayfaring Stranger, Ballads & Folk Songs, Women: Folk Songs About the Fair Sex, Folk Songs Dramatic and Humorous,* and *Christmas Day in the Morning, Wayfaring Stranger, Return of the Wayfaring Stranger, More Folk Songs, American Hymns, The Animal Fair* and *Mother Goose Songs*. The steady, varied stream of albums enabled him to build a large following.

In 1950, Ives's name was listed on the infamous Red Channels pamphlet identifying him as a Communist. Two years later, he cooperated with the House Un-American Activities Committee, which ended his blacklisting and allowed him to continue the many branches of his career. Although like everyone else he had personal political views, the mighty folksinger wasn't going to jeopardize or destroy everything he had worked so hard to achieve.

In 1951, he enjoyed a huge hit with "On Top of Old Smoky," a song which had been a staple of many a folk performer's repertoire. As well, he recorded a number of noncommercial albums for the Encyclopaedia Brittanica files that would later be titled *Historical America in Song*. Although an interesting project, he concentrated more on commercial recordings.

His activity increased during this decade in a variety of fields. Ives published books, acted on Broadway and in the movies, and recorded several albums, including *Coronation Concert, The Wild Side of Life, Men, Down to the Sea in Ships, In the Quiet of the Night, Burl Ives Sings for Fun, Songs of Ireland, Old Time Varieties, Captain Burl Ives' Ark, Australian Folk Songs,* and *Cheers*. By the end of the 1950s, he was on the verge of becoming a household name.

In 1961, despite enjoying a number of folk hits and releasing a large catalog of albums, Ives switched to a more country-oriented sound. He would hit the charts with "A Little Bitty Tear," and "Funny Way of Laughin'," which won him a Grammy. The versatile singer proved that he could handle any material, and in the process enlarged his fan base without alienating already dedicated followers. Despite stiff competition, there was always a special place for his friendly voice in the market.

In the 1960s, he devoted much of his time to appearing in movies. He appeared in and narrated the children's holiday classics, *Santa Claus Is Coming to Town* and *Rudolph the Red-Nosed Reindeer*. He did find time to continue his recording career, and even made an album for the younger set, *Chim Chim Cheree and Other Children's Choices*. Because of his multimedia approach, Ives was able to excel in a variety of areas, unlike other musicians.

By the end of the decade, he was one of the most well-established entertainers in the world and boasted a career on TV and radio, and in the movies and the recording studio. During the protest era, Ives was one of the busiest of all folk artists. Later, he would cut a couple of albums for Columbia, *The Times They Are A-Changin'* and *Softly and Tenderly*.

In 1973, he returned to recording with the country-flavored effort, *Payin' My Dues Again*. His catalog also included children's and religious albums. With his smooth, easy-listening voice, Ives could cut an album in any style and the label was guaranteed to make a profit. However, by the end of the 1970s, he began to slow down. His appearances and recording dates were carefully selected, enabling him to maintain a certain level of popularity.

Eventually, Ives retired and relocated to Washington State. Although he was no longer active, his extensive catalog and reruns of the holiday classics ensured that he remained well-known in the public eye. He was introduced to a new generation and cultivated the positive results of hard work, which spanned a 40-year career. On April 14, 1995, the great folksinger, actor, and recording artist died in Anacortes, Washington.

Burl Ives was a folk music icon. There were many aspects to his career and he conquered each one with his gentle, genuine heart and attitude. As a singer, he recorded more than 100 albums and his catalog includes hundreds of songs. He was an actor who starred in many films as well as on Broadway, and his appearance in the holiday classics cemented a lifelong and posthumous popularity.

Ives was blessed with an unmistakable voice. Just a few notes and his rich, friendly timber was identified. Because of his accessible style, he appealed to listeners of all ages. Add to this a grandfatherly image with a white beard and a solid presence, and it is easy to understand why he was so successful. The burly entertainer managed to parlay his folk singing career into work as a radio personality, as well as on stage and screen.

He recorded hundreds of songs. A short list includes "I Know an Old Lady (Who Swallowed a Fly)," "The Blue Tail Fly," "Big Rock Candy Mountain," "On Top of Old Smoky," "Lavender Blue (Dilly Dilly)," "Silver and Gold," "Frosty the Snowman," "Funny Way of Laughing" "Grandfather Kringle," "Twelve Days of Christmas," "That's My Heart Strings," "The Bus Stop Song," "I'm the Boss," "The Moon Is High," "Salt Water Guitar," "The Story of Bobby Lee Trent," "Evil Off My Mind," "Taste of Heaven," "Gingerbread House," "Tumbleweed Snowman," "The Tail of the Comet Kohoutek," "A Very Fine Lady," "It's Gonna Be a Mixed Up Xmas," "The Christmas Legend of Monkey Joe," "The Night Before Christmas," and "A Little Bitty Tear." Whether singing an original or a cover song, Ives stamped each number with his inimitable, personal style.

He was a first class entertainer. He performed hundreds of concerts, and, because of his versatility, Ives was able to excite audiences of all ages. There was something special in seeing the Wayfarin' Stranger live, on stage. The warm demeanor on his records was greatly amplified in front of an enthusiastic crowd.

Ives first broke into show business with a radio show. Over the years he would appear on a number of programs including the *Wayfarin' Stranger, Back Where I Come From, Burl Ives Coffee Club, The Columbia Workshop, Roadside, The Log of the R-77, The People, Yes, A Child's History of Hot Music, Columbia Presents Corwi, The Lonesome Train, El Capitan and the Corporal, The Theatre Guild on the Air, Sing Out, Sweet Land, Hollywood Star Time, The Return of Frank James, The Burl Ives Show, Hollywood Fights Back, The Kaiser Traveller,* and *Burl Ives Sings.* Because of his instantly recognizable voice, he was successful in any medium.

He appeared in a number of movies, including *East of Eden, Desire Under the Elms, Smoky, Summer Magic, The Brass Bottle, Two Moon Junction, Poor Little Rich Girl: The Barbara Hutton Story, Uphill All the Way, The Ewok Adventure, The First Easter Rabbit, The New Adventures of Heidi, Roots, Baker's Hawk, The McMasters, The Daydreamer, Ensign Pulver, Summer Magic, A Face in the Crowd, So Dear to My Heart, Cat on a Hot Tin Roof,* and *The Big Country.* He won an Academy Award for the latter. He was as fine an actor as he was a singer.

While he was solid in these roles, it is his later casting as the narrator in the all-time classic Christmas specials, *Rudolph the Red-Nosed Reindeer* and *Santa Claus Is Coming to Town,* for which he is best remembered, by at least two generations of children. Every holiday season he is viewed by a new group, which expands his already broad appeal. Ives also appeared on TV shows, including a production of *Pinocchio, Playhouse 90, Caravan of Courage: An Ewok Adventure, O.K. Crackerby* and *The Bold Ones: The Lawyers.*

He was a well-known stage actor appearing in *Pocohontas Preferred, The*

Boys from Syracuse, Heavenly Express, This Is the Army, Sing Out Sweet Land, Paint Your Wagon, She Stoops to Conquer, Knickerbocker Holiday, The Man Who Came to Dinner, Show Boat, and *Dr. Cook's Garden.* However, his most famous role was as the notorious Big Daddy in *Cat on a Hot Tin Roof.* Rumors persist that playwright Tennessee Williams had Ives in mind when he created the character.

Ives was also an author. In 1948, he wrote his autobiography, *The Wayfarin' Stranger.* He would also publish *Burl Ives Song Book; Tales of America; Sea Songs of Sailing, Whaling and Fishing;* and *The Wayfaring Stranger's Notebook.* Although his written work never brought him the same popularity as his song catalog or acting roles, it was a dimension of his talent that was well represented.

Ives was a political activist, but not a visible one. While he was known to be sympathetic to many causes and was seen in public with radicals such as Pete Seeger, Woody Guthrie, Cisco Houston, Lee Hays, Ronnie Gilbert and Fred Hellerman, he managed to walk a tightrope. He was skilled at voicing his opinion without incurring the wrath of the authorities.

Burl Ives was a true American songster. He delivered at least a dozen songs which remain classics. His acting career on TV, in films and on Broadway made him hugely popular. The burly, gentle man always had a song in his heart, a Wayfarin' Stranger who entertained audiences then and now.

DISCOGRAPHY:

Burl Ives, Decca 711.
Ballads Folk and Country Songs, Decca DL 5093.
Ballads and Folk Songs, Vol. 1, Decca DL-5013.
Ballads and Folk Songs, Vol. 2, Decca DL-5080.
Lonesome Train: A Musical Legend, Decca 5054.
Christmas Day in the Morning, Decca D -5428.
Folk Songs Dramatic and Dangerous, Decca 5467.
Women: Folk Songs About the Fair Sex, Decca 5490.
Burl Ives Sings for Fun, Decca D-8248.
Coronation Concert [live], Decca D-8080.
Down to the Sea in Ships, Decca D-8245.
In the Quiet of the Night, Decca D-8247.
Men, Decca D-8125.
Women, Decca D-8246.
Christmas Eve with Burl Ives [1957], Decca D-8391.
Australian Folk Songs, Decca D-8749.
Captain Burl Ives' Ark, Decca D-8587.
Songs of Ireland, Decca D-8444.
Ballads with Guitar, United Artists 6060.
It's Just My Funny Way of Laughin', Decca 4279.
The Versatile Burl Ives!, Decca 4152.
Scouting Along with Burl Ives, Columbia 347.

Chim Chim Cheree and Other Children's Choices, Disney 60410.
Have a Holly Jolly Christmas, MCA MCA-15002.
Sings the Great Country Hits, Decca 74973.
The Times They Are A-Changin' [CBS], CBS PCT-9675.
Song Book, MCA Coral 20029.
Favorites for Children, Shout Factory 8266631105.
Rudolph the Red-Nosed Reindeer, MCA 15003.
Santa Claus Is Coming to Town, MCA MCAC-15030.
Burl Ives Sings, CBS CK-33183.
How Great Thou Art, Echo 3
Songs I Sang in Sunday School, Echo 2.
Christmas at the White House, Caedmon CDS-1415.
Little White Duck and Other Children's Favorites, CBS 31183.
Pearly Shells, Decca 74578.
The Wayfaring Stranger, Collectables 6474.
Return of the Wayfaring Stranger, Collectables 6662.
Burl Ives Presents America's Musical Heritage, Longines 195.
The Best of Burl's for Boys and Girls, MCA 98.
The Best of Burl Ives, MCA 4034.
At His Best, Essex 4813.
A Little Bitty Tear [Universal], Universal Special Products 20280.
A Little Bitty Tear: The Nashville Years 1961–1965, Bear Family 15667.
Christmas Album [Columbia/Legacy], Sony 64771.
In Memorium, Legacy 418.
Greatest Hits, MCA 114.
Poor Wayfaring Stranger, Pearl 7090.
More of the Best, Delta 12650.
Some of the Best, Delta 12649.
Sings His Favorites, Collector's Edition 7.
A Little Bitty Tear: The Best of Burl Ives, MCA 6.
A Little Bitty Tear [Prism] [live], Prism Leisure 124.
Burl Ives [Compilation], A World of Music 12533.
Christmas Album, Sony Special Products 13349.
A Twinkle in Your Eye, Sony Wonder 63420.
On Top of Old Smoky, Sony 28541.
Sings the Biggest Christmas Hits, Universal Special Products 21015.
Christmas Eve with Burl Ives [1998], Universal Special Products 21071.
Another Day Another Year, Hallmark 31114.
The Very Best of Burl Ives Christmas, MCA 12018.
Inspirational Favorites, Universal Special Products 112108.
I'm Goin' Away, Columbia River 140000.
Lavender Blue: Songs of Charm, Humor and Sincerity, Jasmine 2524.
We'll Meet Again, Word 2.
20 Gospel Favorites, Madacy 741.
The Times They Are A-Changin,' Madacy 168.
The Collection, EMI 5763232.
20th Century Masters—The Millennium Collection: The Best of Burl Ives, MCA 112656.
Collection, MRA 084.

Best of Burl Ives: 20th Century Masters/The Christmas Collection, MCA 000051903.
Members Edition, United Multi License 53086.
Troubadour, Naxos Nostalgia 8120728.
Burl Ives, Platinum Disc 3270.
The Wayfaring Stranger, ASV/Living Era 5543.
Burl Ives [Platinum Disc 2 CD], Platinum Disc 14.
Genius of Folk, St. Clair 6584.
30 Great Performances, Dove 7142.
Wild Side of Life, Platinum 1416.
The Best of Burl Ives: Little Bitty Tear, Collectables 847.
The Singing Wayfarer, Primo 6048.
Songs from the Big Rock Candy Mountain, Revola 216.
Blue Tail Fly, Dynamic Entertainment 2961.
Christmas & Hits Duos, Geffen 111331.
The Best of Burl Ives, Vol. 2, MCA 4089.

Earl Robinson (1910–1991)

Ballad for Americans

The welding of folk music with politics added a new dimension to the genre, but didn't raise its popularity level. In fact, if anything, it decreased acceptance in different quarters because often the artists were linked to communism, which stands in opposition to the democracy that is the foundation of the United States. However, many of these musicians forged on because of their belief that they could use their music as a tool for change and social justice, including the man who gave the world his ballad for Americans. His name was Earl Robinson.

Earl Hawley Robinson was born on July 2, 1910, in Seattle, Washington. He began a musical career at an early age and studied the violin as his principal instrument. Later he added the piano. The youth's love of music continued into his teens and early twenties. Robinson majored in composition at the University of Washington and received a B.A. and a teaching certificate.

After graduation in 1933, Robinson, young and idealistic, decided to travel and experience the world. He ventured to China, where he remained for some time before working his way back to the United States by playing piano on an ocean liner. The journey would have a profound effect on his writing as well as his social and political points of view. He had seen the tough circumstances people dealt with in countries without a constitution.

At this time Robinson was forming his personal political beliefs and considered himself a left-wing activist. He joined the Young Communist League and the Workers Laboratory Theater, which would later become the Theater of Action. It was here that he composed the song "Joe Hill," about the famous union leader, radical, and folk musician who inspired a generation, despite meeting with an early demise at the hands of the authorities.

In 1934, Robinson moved across the country to New York to study with Hanns Eisler and Aaron Copland. In 1936, he spent time with the WPA Federal Theatre Workshop, as well as becoming musical director at the Communist Run Camp Unit. He led the People's Chorus at the International Workers Order. A staunch opponent of fascism, the blossoming songwriter used his musical skills to fight that political system.

In 1939 he continued to write material including "Ballad for Americans," which would become his signature song. It was utilized in the play *Sing for Your Supper*. That same year, the Works Progress Administration was cancelled and CBS picked up the number as an opening for its *Pursuit of Happiness* radio program. When Paul Robeson cut a version it became a smash hit and enabled Robinson to record with his group, American People's Chorus.

The song, "Ballad for Americans," was praised in different quarters and earned Robinson a Guggenheim fellowship to write a musical adaptation of Carl Sandburg's work, *The People, Yes.* When Eleanor Roosevelt heard the song she invited him to perform at some of her political events. The song opened many doors and Robinson took advantage of the opportunities that came his way.

Throughout the 1940s, he expanded his work to include scores for television, theater, radio and film, the latter proving very lucrative and showing that he possessed a considerable amount of talent. He wrote songs for the films *Romance of Rose Ridge* and *California*. Because of his association with the first family, Robinson was given the license to compose a musical score for the documentary *The Roosevelt Story*. He also was involved in the project *Giants in the Land,* a movie about General Motors.

He continued to earn a comfortable living in Hollywood until the McCarthy era destroyed his career. The author of "Ballad for Americans" was blacklisted and when the opportunities in Los Angeles dried up he returned to New York. There Robinson scratched out an existence by composing a folk opera, *Sandbag,* but because of the heavy scrutiny he was under it got little attention.

Robinson found more work when the McCarthy era came to an end. He composed a concerto for the banjo as well as a piano suite entitled *The New Human*. His signature tune, "Ballad for Americans" continued to earn him modest royalties, especially after the popular crooner Bing Crosby recorded a version. By this time the number had become a folk standard and many artists included it in their repertoires.

After a decade of financial struggle, Robinson found steady work as a teacher. From 1957 to the mid–1960s, he taught at the Elisabeth Irwin High School in New York, where the clever writer directed the chorus and orchestra, providing them with established and personal material, including his famous "Ballad for Americans." In the early 1960s, the Greenwich Village Symphony Orchestra recorded its own version of the well-known song.

In 1966, Robinson left the high school and moved back to California, where he conducted the Extension Chorus at the University of California for a couple of years. In 1969, he re-entered television, composing songs for *The Great Man's Whiskers* and *The Adventures of Huckleberry Finn*. Because of his strong writing skills, he was never out of work for long.

Throughout the 1970s and into the next decade, Robinson continued to teach and compose for various TV shows. In 1989, after retiring, he moved back to Seattle, Washington, where he worked on his various personal projects until July 20, 1991, when he was killed in an automobile accident. He was 81 years old.

Earl Robinson was another controversial folk artist. While a proven musician and songwriter, he was probably better known in some circles for his left-wing politics. There were many aspects to his career and in order to truly understand the man, one must look at the complete profile.

Robinson was more than just a songwriter. He composed material considered anthems, including the labor ballad "I Dreamed I Saw Joe Hill Last Night." Joe Hill, the notorious fighter for the common worker was the embodiment of the protest spirit. Paul Robeson and Joan Baez are just two of the many artists who produced interesting cover versions of the song.

Robinson wrote other politically-charged tunes including "Abe Lincoln," "The House I Live In," and "Hurry Sundown." He also penned "Black and White," which Three Dog Night later covered when racial tensions in the United States were still strong. Thirty years later the song retains its message of unity, harmony, peace and racial tolerance. Robinson saw everyone as equal.

Despite a healthy catalog of songs, his most famous song was "Ballad for Americans," a cantata which Paul Robeson performed as a soloist. It was the essence of the message Robinson was trying to put across to the world. Another tour de force was "The Lonesome Train." His compositions underscored documentaries including *The House I Live In* starring Frank Sinatra, which won an Academy Award.

Film scores were another important part of his creative output. A short list includes *The House I Live In, A Walk in the Sun, The Roosevelt Story, California,* and *Romance of Roxy Ridge,* among others. In the 1940s, Robinson established a comfortable living composing for Hollywood until the blacklisting wiped him out.

Robinson was among the leftist folk musicians of the twentieth century, people like Joan Baez, Woody Guthrie, Ronnie Gilbert, Leadbelly, Josh White, Fred Hellerman, Joe Glazer, Paul Robeson, Carl Sandburg and Pete Seeger. Much of his material was written to help the downtrodden, and to support causes that needed a spokesman.

Robinson left his mark in another way. His son Perry was a noted clarinet player who attempted to establish himself as an avant-garde leader. He would go on to play with Paul Bley, Archie Shepp, Bill Dixon, Roswell Rudd, Gunter Hampel and eventually in Dave Brubeck's Two Generations of Brubeck. Although he followed a much different path than his father, Perry Robinson also made an impact on American music.

In 1989, a revue of his music occurred at the Pioneer Square Theatre in his hometown of Seattle, which provided an interesting and reflective look back at his varied career. At this point in time, he was recognized as one of the architects of the folk music revival that occurred in the late 1950s.

Robinson was a political folkie of the highest order. He wrote about pain and suffering through the eyes of someone who lived the life. He was always most interested in helping others and is well-remembered as the composer of the "Ballad for Americans."

DISCOGRAPHY:

A Walk in the Sun and Other Songs and Ballads, Smithsonian Folkways 2324.
Earl Robinson Sings, Smithsonian Folkways 3545.
Alive and Well, Aspen 3010.
The Only Way, Jet Star 5021272060122.

Woody Guthrie (1912–1967)
Bound for Glory

In every style one figure is the supreme pioneer, the leader that all others hold up as their mentor. Although many great performers throughout the history of American and international folk music deserve special recognition, one name stands out from the early days. It was evident he was bound for glory. His name was Woody Guthrie.

Woodrow Wilson Guthrie was born on July 14, 1912, in Okemah, Oklahoma. His political connections began at an early age; he was named for the 28th president of the United States, Woodrow Wilson. As well, Guthrie's father, Charley Edward, was a politician who held an elective post as district court clerk. But it was his mother, Nora Belle (Tanner), who taught him folksongs. Tragedy struck the family when Guthrie's sister burned to death, which had a profound impact on him.

From an early age, young Guthrie developed a decided interest in music. His first instrument was the harmonica and he became proficient enough to play in front of an audience. Later he picked up the guitar and became a double threat. Guthrie cut his teeth on folk standards like "Oh, Susanna," "Camptown Races," "Swanee River," "Michael Row the Boat to Shore," "Tom Dooley," "Jeannie with the Light Brown Hair," "Nelly Was a Lady," "Nelly Bly," "My Old Kentucky Home," "Old Dog Tray," "Hard Times Come Again No More," "Lou'siana Belle," "The Voice of Bygone Days," "Lily Ray," "Angelina Baker," and "Beautiful Dreamer," among others.

In 1927, fifteen-year-old Guthrie would watch his family be destroyed in the span of two days. His father suffered a debilitating injury as the result of a kerosene accident. Two days later his mother, who had been diagnosed with Huntington's disease, an illness affecting mental and muscle control, was committed to an insane asylum. She would die three years later.

These two events led to his quick maturation as a singing artist. He remained with an older brother and family friends, but his activities went unsupervised, enabling him to hitchhike around the Gulf Coast states, working at odd jobs to see him through his journey. It was at this point that he began to collect the raw material that would find its way into the cycle of songs that would someday make him a legend.

He quit high school in the tenth grade to focus on a musical career. Guthrie joined his father in Pampa, Texas, where the elder Guthrie had gone to recover from his severe burns. While in Texas, Guthrie formed his first professional band with Matt Jennings and Cluster Baker. They called themselves the Corncob Trio. In 1933, he married Mary Esta Jennings, his partner's sister.

One of the aspects that set Guthrie apart from other folksingers was his dedication to songwriting. His early material focused on tragic, natural events, like the major dust storm that hit Pampa and brought economic strain across the Great Plains. His voice was a beacon in very difficult times and the song "Dusty Old Dust" was a satiric observation on the suffering of ordinary Americans.

In 1935, he self-published his initial collection in a songbook that would form the foundation of the folk music teaching across the country and later around the world. Despite the joy of welcoming his first child into the world, Guthrie was a man on a mission and embraced the life of a train-hopping hobo to spread his message across the country. His adventures inspired more ideas for future songs.

In 1937, he moved to California, leaving behind a family that now numbered two girls. He teamed up with his cousin Leon Jerry "Oklahoma Jack" and the duo performed on *The Oklahoma and Woody Show* on radio station KFVO in Los Angeles. When his cousin quit, Guthrie recruited Maxine Crissman, whom he nicknamed "Lefty Lou" and the show was renamed *The Woody and Lefty Lou Show.*

The Dust Bowl, the event that had wiped out farming in America's heartland, was a rich vein of musical inspiration that Guthrie mined with expertise. "Do Re Mi," "Oklahoma Hills," and "Philadelphia Lawyer" made him the voice of the common folk and enabled Guthrie to earn a decent enough living that he could send for his wife and two children to join him.

Guthrie would take a break from the radio show to travel throughout the country once again. He returned to KFVO re-inspired by the pain of the struggling migrant workers. His songs took on a more political aspect, like "Pretty Boy Floyd" and "Vigilante Man." He also expanded his efforts with a column "Woody Sez" that appeared in the Communist paper *People's World.*

In October 1939, he added a son to his growing family. Guthrie left his radio show and returned to Texas before pushing on to New York City, where he hooked up with actor and friend, Will Geer. The latter was appearing in the Broadway musical *Tobacco Road.* While listening to Kate Smith's rendition of "God Bless America," Guthrie was inspired to write his own patriotic song, initially titled "God Blessed America for Me." The song would evolve into "This Land Is Your Land," and although he is credited with many important numbers, this anthem would become his most famous.

By 1940, the sad fortunes of the Okies, the Midwestern farmers who had lost their farms and headed west to become migrant workers, had been well-documented, mainly due to the *Grapes of Wrath*, John Steinbeck's best-selling novel, which was later turned into a movie. Guthrie, a well-seasoned traveler, had met Steinbeck, who asked him to perform at the Forrest Theatre in a benefit for migrant workers. Seemingly overnight, Guthrie was catapulted into the spotlight as a national spokesman for the plight of the downtrodden people from Oklahoma.

The performance at the Forrest Theatre was vital because there he was introduced to Leadbelly, Pete Seeger, Aunt Molly Jackson, and, most importantly, Alan Lomax. The latter was the assistant in charge of the Archive of Folksong at the Library of Congress. He would be a tremendous help to Guthrie.

Lomax invited Guthrie to Washington, D.C., and interviewed him for the archive. Guthrie sounded like a cross between Jimmie Rodgers, the father of country music, and cowboy/actor/crooner Will Rogers. For the Library of Congress, he cut some of his famous songs including "So Long It's Been Good to Know Yuh," "Do Re Mi," "Pretty Boy Floyd," "I Ain't Got No Home," "Worried Man Blues," and "Goin' Down That Road Feeling Bad." In 1964, at the height of the folk boom, they would be released in a three-LP box set.

Guthrie, on the request of Lomax, appeared on the nationally broadcast CBS radio program *Columbia School of the Air,* and later on *The Pursuit of Happiness.* Lomax was also instrumental in helping Guthrie get a recording contract with RCA Victor that resulted in two very influential albums, *Dust Bowl Ballads, Vol. 1 and Dust Bowl Ballads, Vol. 2.* The albums included many of the songs that were recorded for the Library of Congress and a new number, "Tom Joad," a reference to the novel, *The Grapes of Wrath.*

Guthrie returned to the Southwest with his friend Pete Seeger for some time before he moved on to New York to appear on the CBS radio show, *Back Where I Come From,* another Lomax program. He teamed up with good friend Cisco Houston to perform at various night clubs. He sent for his family, who moved across the country to be with him in the Big Apple, only to relocate to California not long after. He appeared on the program *Pipe Smoking Time.*

By this time, Guthrie was famous enough for the Bonneville Power Administration, part of the Department of the Interior in Portland, Oregon, to commission him to sing and narrate songs for a documentary on the building of the Grand Coulee Dam. He would contribute some 26 tunes, including "Roll on Columbia," "Grand Coulee Dam," and "Pastures of Plenty."

After the project was completed, Guthrie returned to New York and formed the Almanac Singers with Seeger, Lee Hays and Millard Lampell. The musical group's strong political message was evident in the albums *Deep Sea Chanteys and Sodbuster Ballads,* recorded on the General Records label. They toured at union gatherings throughout the country. Around this time, Guthrie was briefly reunited with his family, but his wife had suffered enough of the absenteeism, and separated from him, moving the children to El Paso, Texas.

The Almanac Singers suffered through line-up changes, but continued to record and perform. Guthrie, the chief songwriter for the group, wrote social numbers like the "Sinking of the Reuben James" the story of a U.S. destroyer torpedoed by German U-boats. The group declared itself pro-war after the Pearl Harbor incident. Guthrie, who had often clashed with government ideology, was on the same side as Uncle Sam.

The group appeared on many radio shows, including *This Is War,* broadcast across the nation. However, because of their political affiliations they were not booked in traditional halls and even turned down offers to perform in well-known venues. Nightclub dates and a recording contract with Decca Records were cancelled because they were tied to the Communist Party.

On a personal note, he met Marjorie Greenblatt Mazia and had an affair with her, despite still being married. She was a dancer with the Martha Graham dance troupe and was also married. The two would have a daughter. Guthrie broke away from the Almanac Singers after more than a year, and formed the Headline Singers, which included Leadbelly, Sonny Terry and Brownie McGhee.

In 1943, *Bound for Glory*, Guthrie's autobiography, appeared. Soon after, his first wife divorced him, making him eligible for the draft. He joined the Merchant Marines and undertook the dangerous task of carrying supplies for the invasion of Italy; his good friend Cisco Houston was on the same trip. They served proudly on two more missions for their country.

In 1944, Guthrie signed with the Asch Record Company. He cut hundreds of songs over the years and Houston, Sonny Terry, Leadbelly and Bess Hawes, a former member of the Almanac Singers, often backed him in the studio. One of the songs was "This Land Is Your Land." At the time, many of the sides were not released because Asch was too small a label to handle the wealth of material.

After another war excursion that ended in England, Guthrie appeared briefly on the BBC before returning home. Some time later, Asch began releasing a number of Guthrie's songs on various albums including *Folksay: American Ballads and Dances* and *Blues*. Finally, a solo work entitled *Woody Guthrie,* a three-record collection which included such songs as "Grand Coulee Dam" and "Jesus Christ," appeared. Guthrie performed on the radio show *Ballad Gazette,* where his signature tune "This Land Is Your Land" served as the theme song, as well as the NBC program *America for Christmas.*

His recording progress was halted when he no longer qualified for the Merchant Marines and was forced to enlist in the Army. Guthrie was stationed at various locations around the country to wait out the rest of the war, which was rapidly coming to an end. While serving time at one of the bases, he heard a song, "Oklahoma Hills," on the radio, credited to Jack Guthrie. After some legal discussions, Guthrie was given co-credit so he could receive royalties.

He married Marjorie Mazia just before being discharged from the Army. Guthrie resumed his musical career recording for Asch, which released the album *Struggle: Documentary #1.* He was later asked to write a series of songs about Sacoo and Vanzetti, two migrant anarchists executed for a robbery and the murder of two guards. On the performance side of his career, he played concerts under the auspices of an organization called People's Songs, an outfit designed to promote political folk material.

During this period, he recorded tunes for his children which would be packaged as *Songs to Grow On: Nursery Days.* In 1947, the album *Work Songs to Grow On* was released. Sadly, Guthrie's daughter Cathy, the initial inspiration for much of his output during this period, died in a fire early that year, which had a profound effect on Guthrie.

Arguably, at this point he had ceased being a national entertainer and was more of a rambling folksinger. But his name remained prominent in different venues. For example, the musical *Finian's Rainbow* opened on Broadway for a run of more than 700 performances. Sonny Terry, the blues-folksinger, acted in the show that included a character named Woody, modeled after Guthrie. The character was a free-spirited, guitar-playing, ex-merchant seaman who helped create a labor revolt.

Guthrie had a fifth child, Arlo Davy, who would become a prominent singer-songwriter and would forever be immortalized by the signature song "Alice's Restaurant," a perennial favorite on the American Thanksgiving. He would both escape and extend his father's legacy. Joady Ben Guthrie also became a performer. A couple of years later, daughter Nora Lee, Guthrie's seventh child, entered the world.

Guthrie continued to record, reworking much of the material from his earlier output. In 1947, the Asch label went bankrupt, which dealt a severe blow to Guthrie's career. However, Moses Asch's partner, Herbert Harris, held onto some of the master recordings as well as a pressing plant that he would sell to Pickwick Records. In the 1960s, a major selection of Guthrie's catalog would be issued on the Pickwick Everest label.

In the late 1940s, Guthrie's greatest fear — that he would inherit Huntington's disease which had crippled his mother — materialized into reality. But since his behavior had always been so different, the early signs were not detected, and many attributed his off-the-wall actions to alcoholism. His last major composition, "Deportee," a song written on behalf of the migrant workers who perished in an airplane crash, was released.

His career received a much-needed infusion when others began to record his songs. The Maddox Brothers & Rose hit the charts with "Philadelphia Lawyer," and the Weavers, a group which included Pete Seeger and Lee Hays (formerly of the Almanac Singers), recorded "So Long It's Been Good to Know Yuh," which peaked in the top five of the pop charts. Suddenly, Guthrie was back in the spotlight.

By 1951, Guthrie's personal life started to unravel as the problems continued to mount. His wife separated from him due to his erratic behavior. The once-sharp musical skills had deteriorated and when he tried to record for Decca the sessions were cancelled. In 1952, while in the hospital, he was diagnosed with Huntington's.

He moved to California and met the much-younger art student Anneke van Kirk Marshall. The two traveled to New York and then on to Florida, where Guthrie suffered a crippling injury to his right arm in a campfire accident. After another divorce, he married the 20-year-old Marshall and they relocated to New York. A year later, Guthrie welcomed his eighth child into the world — a daughter, Lorina Lynn. Sometime later the couple split up and the infant was put up for adoption.

In the fall of 1954, Guthrie checked himself into the Brooklyn State Hospital, and on the weekends rekindled his relationship with Marjorie Mazia, whom he had divorced in order to marry Marshall. In the spring of 1956, he was arrested for vagrancy in New Jersey and committed to Greystone Park

Hospital, where he remained for five years. He would later be moved to the Brooklyn facility.

Ironically, while his physical condition worsened, his popularity soared. The Weavers, who had disbanded, later reunited and performed "This Land Is Your Land." A benefit concert for Guthrie's children was held at the Pythian Hall in New York City, and although Guthrie was in attendance that night, he didn't perform. More importantly, the event was one of the initiating forces behind the folk boom.

When groups like the Kingston Trio recorded a cover version of "Hard, Ain't It Hard," which was included on their gold self-titled album, it only enhanced Guthrie's popularity. Later they would cover "Hard Travelin'," "This Land Is Your Land," "Pastures of Plenty" and "Deportee." The New Christy Minstrels also cut a version of "This Land Is Your Land" that reached the pop charts. In 1962, *Dust Bowl Ballads* was reissued as an LP. In 1964, the Library of Congress Recordings were released and nominated for a Grammy Award for Best Folk Recording. During this period, songbooks were published and *Born to Win,* a collection of Guthrie's writings, was also made available.

In 1966, at the height of Bob Dylan's career, Guthrie was moved to Creedmore State Hospital in Queens, New York. On October 3, 1967, Woody Guthrie, the ragamuffin singer-songwriter, protester, and champion of the poor, hard-working, average American, died.

Woody Guthrie was the prime architect of the folk music movement during the 1930s and 1940s. He was the centerpiece of the entire style and his influence is immeasurable. There was a distinct individuality to his songs, lyrics and experiences that inspired hundreds of performers.

He was never a master musician but was handy with the guitar and could play a steady harmonica. More importantly, he was able to bring all of his musical talents together in one concise, commercial and meaningful package. He created harmonies and melodies that were not difficult to play, which enabled many to cover his material. Sadly, the instrumental side of his songs has often been overlooked because of their strong lyrical impact.

There was a definite charm to his homespun vocal delivery. There was no mistaking his roots but he never came across as an uneducated wanderer. Instead he seemed a traveler with rich experiences and stories to tell. The rhythmic appeal of his voice was catchy and accompanied by his solid instrumental abilities was pleasing. His distinct utterance was the soundtrack of a generation and many singers tried to emulate it.

Scarcely a folksinger has not recorded at least one Guthrie song or performed his material on stage. He influenced hundreds of artists. A partial list includes Bob Dylan, Arlo Guthrie, Richie Havens, Odetta, Pete Seeger, Tom Paxton, Joan Baez, Tom Rush, Ramblin' Jack Elliott, Country Joe McDonald, Cisco Houston, Utah Phillips, and dozens more. His impact spilled into other styles including rock-and-roll and pop.

Although he was a popular performer and regarded as the leader of the folk movement, he was an irritation to the establishment for many years. He was linked to communism, protests, union strikes, and disturbances and was considered a troublemaker, a radical in the eyes of the authorities. His rebelliousness is as much part of his legend as his songs, musical abilities and performances.

After his death there were two all-star tributes. One was held in New York and included performances by Judy Collins, Bob Dylan, Arlo Guthrie, Richie Havens, Odetta, Pete Seeger and Tom Paxton, among others. The proceeds went to benefit research on Huntington's disease. The second concert was held at the Hollywood Bowl and featured the same cast of performers with the addition of Country Joe McDonald and Ramblin' Jack Elliott. Two years later, albums celebrating both events were released and made it into the charts.

During the 1970s, Guthrie's popularity remained intact. A book of his newspaper columns entitled *Woody Sez* was published and a year later *Seeds of Man*, the story of a hunt with his father for a lost gold mine also appeared. His autobiography, *Bound for Glory*, was made into a movie, which enabled him to stay fresh in the public's mind.

The tributes continued long after his demise. In 1977, he was inducted into the Nashville Songwriter's Hall of Fame. Eleven years later he was inducted into the Rock and Roll Hall of Fame because of his influence on Dylan and a number of folk-rock acts like the Byrds, the Eagles, Poco, the Band, and many others. In 1979, an off–Broadway musical appeared that featured his name.

When Moses Asch, the founder of the label died, the archives of Folkways Records were donated to the Smithsonian Institution. This spurred a number of releases, including greatest hits packages. An all-star album of songs by Guthrie and Leadbelly, *Folkways: A Vision Shared*, was released and featured performances by Bob Dylan, Willie Nelson, U2, Bruce Springsteen and John Mellencamp.

In 1989, "This Land Is Your Land" was inducted into the Grammy Hall of Fame. A year later, another book of Guthrie's writings, *Pastures of Plenty: A Self-Portrait—The Unpublished Writings of an American Folk Hero*, was released. In 1991, another musical based on his life opened. In 1998, *Mermaid Avenue*, a series of unpublished lyrics, was issued as Billy Bragg and Wilco combined to unearth the Guthrie files. In 2000, a second volume was released, and, like the first one, made it into the charts. The reissue of Guthrie's music continued and like so many other figures who have passed away, his recordings are continually repackaged for profit.

Woody Guthrie was a genuine folksinger who was able to instill his songs into the national psyche. He was a true American who was consistently interested in improving conditions for the less fortunate. Despite many obstacles during his life, there never seemed to be a doubt that he was bound for glory.

DISCOGRAPHY:

Anglo-American Ballads, Volume 1, Rounder 1511.

The Ballad Hunter, Parts I and II, Library of Congress Recording Laboratory AFS L49.

The Ballad Hunter, Parts III and IV, Library of Congress Recording Laboratory AFS L50.

The Ballad Hunter, Parts V and VI, Library of Congress Recording Laboratory AFS L51.

Buffalo Skinners: The Asch Recordings Volume 4, Smithsonian Folkways SF 40103.

The Concert and Radio Series: The Ballad Operas: The Martins and the Coys, Rounder CD 1819.

Dust Bowl Ballads, Rounder 1040.

Hard Travelin': The Asch Recordings Volume 3, Smithsonian Folkways SF 40102.

Muleskinner Blues: The Asch Recordings Volume 2, Smithsonian Folkways CD 40101.

Songs to Grow On for Mother and Child, Smithsonian Folkways SF 45935.

Struggle, Smithsonian Folkways SF 40025.

That's Why We're Marching: World War II and the American Folk Song Movement, Smithsonian Folkways SF 40021.

This Land Is Your Land: The Asch Recordings Volume 1, Smithsonian Folkways SFW 40100.

Woody Guthrie: Columbia River Collection, Rounder 1036.

Woody Guthrie: Library of Congress Recordings, Rounder 1041–1043.

Talking Dust Bowl, Smithsonian Folkways FA-2011.

Bound for Glory, Smithsonian Folkways 2481.

Nursery Days, Smithsonian Folkways 7675.

Woody Guthrie Sings Folk Songs, Smithsonian Folkways 2483.

Woody Guthrie Sings Folk Songs, Vol. 2, Smithsonian Folkways 2484.

Dust Bowl Ballads, Budha 99724.

One of a Kind, Pair 1294.

Bonneville Dam and Other Columbia River Songs, Verve Folkways 9036.

Songs from Bound to Glory, Warner Bros. 56335.

Poor Boy, Xtra 1067.

Worried Man Blues, Special Music Company 4824.

Grow Big Songs, Warner Bros. 45021.

Grow Big Songs, Warner Bros. 45022.

The Science of Sound, Smithsonian Folkways 45038.

We Ain't Down Yet!, Cream 1002.

Ballads of Sacco & Venzetti, Smithsonian Folkways 5485.

This Land Is Your Land, Memo 6001.

900 Miles, Public Demand 60542.

Great Dust Storm, Pazzazz 077.

Chain Gangs, Stinson 37.

Cowboy Songs, Stinson 32.
Folk Songs, Vol. 1, Stinson 44.
Songs to Grow On, Vol. 3: This Land Is My Land, Smithsonian Folkways 7027.
Why, Oh, Why, Smithsonian Folkways 45035/6.
More Songs, Vol. 2, Stinson 53.
Dust Bowl Ballads, Folkways 5212.
Library of Congress Recordings, Vols. 1–3, Rounder 1041.
The Early Years, Legacy/Columbia 345.
Woody Guthrie, Everest 204.
Woody Guthrie, Xtra 1012.
This Land Is Your Land, Smithsonian Folkways 31001.
The Greatest Songs of Woody Guthrie, Vanguard 35.
Immortal, Olympic 7101.
Songs to Grow On, Smithsonian Folkways FC-7015.
Woody Guthrie, Vol. 1, CS International Joker 3960.
Woody Guthrie, Vol. 2, CS International Joker 3961.
Collection, Deja Vu 2138.
Library of Congress Recordings, Vol. 2, Rounder 1042.
Library of Congress Recordings, Vol. 3, Rounder 1043.
Immortal: Golden Classics, Pt. 2, Collectables COL-5098.
Long Ways to Travel: The Unreleased Folkways Masters, 1944–1949, Smithsonian
    Folkways 40046.
Woody Guthrie & Cisco Houston, Vols. 1–2, Collectables 5605.
A Legendary Performer, RCA 17742.
Early Masters, Rykodisc/Tradition 1017.
Folk Hero, Collector's Edition 5.
This Land Is Your Land: The Asch Recordings, Vol. 1, Smithsonian Folkways 40100.
This Land Is Your Land: An All American Children's Folk Classic, Rounder 8050.
Woody Guthrie: Members Edition, Members Edition 3024.
Pastures of Plenty, Prism Leisure 427.
Ramblin' Round, Recall 311.
Dust Can't Kill Me, Performance 38277.
Original Folkways Recordings, Mastersong 503723.
The Early Years, Chrisly 40005.
Very Best of Woody Guthrie, Import 29067.
Dust Bowl Ballads, BMG International Camden 57839.
This Machine Kills Fascists, Hallmark 31214.
Very Best of Woody Guthrie, Purple Pyramid 1021.
Hard Luck Blues, Catfish 199.
The Ultimate Collection, Prime Leisure 2234.
Members Edition, Members Edition 30243.
Deja Vu Retro Gold, Retro Music 4237.
Legendary Woody Guthrie, Tradition 2058.
Hard Travelin', Prism Leisure 906.
House of the Rising Sun, Delta 6255.
The Folk Collection, Collectables 2870.
Best of the War Years, Stardust 1290.
Country & Folk Blues, Castle Pulse 652.
A Proper Introduction to Woody Guthrie: This Land Is Your Land, Proper 2059.

This Land Is Your Land, Falcon Home Ent. 3871.
American Folk Legend, Golden Stars 5409.

Lee Hays (1914–1981)
Lonesome Traveler

The connection between folk and political ideologies entrenched the genre even more as the music of the common person. When musicians began to use their songs to bring about change and social justice, folk music began to have a position of responsibility. Each succeeding generation had to ensure this sacred trust. One of those who helped in that regard was Lee Hays, the lonesome traveler.

Lee Elhardt Hays was born on March 14, 1914, in Little Rock, Arkansas. His father was a preacher and moved his family to various parishes in Arkansas and Georgia. Hays participated in the choir at his father's churches. However, the most significant events of his childhood that would shape his political views and career ambitions were the public lynchings of African Americans.

His father's fundamentalist religion also shaped Hays's outlook on the world. He spent his life rebelling against those hardcore values. For example, he started to smoke and drink at an early age, and carried on throughout adulthood. Interestingly, despite shunning his father's religious point of view, Hays's songs had a deep spiritual feel.

During the Great Depression, Hays attended Commonwealth College in Arkansas and formulated a worldview which included universal brotherhood on a planet where all people were created equally. He branched out and became a writer, producing stories, plays and songs. He also preached in local churches and could have followed in his father's footsteps.

But Hays had a greater calling in life: he wanted to utilize his musical talents to bring about social justice, overcoming racism, inequality and violence in society. The budding musician understood the power of song, and folk music was perfectly suited to his ambitions. The idealistic youth needed a vehicle and found it in the unions.

In the 1930s, he left college and started a career as a union activist. The young troubadour found a teaching position at the Highlander Folk School in Tennessee, and worked there for some time. Later, he relocated to New York City, where he furthered his career when he met others in his field, including Pete Seeger, Woody Guthrie, Huddie Ledbetter, Cisco Houston,

Burl Ives and Josh White. But it was in 1941, when he joined the Almanac Singers, that Hays truly came into his own as a folksinger.

He had been writing songs for some time and some of his more popular tunes — "Which Side Are You On?," "Plow the Fourth Bay Under," and "Get Thee Behind Me, Satan" — became staples the group performed at union halls and strike meetings throughout the country. One of his composition strategies was to utilize the tunes of popular Christian hymns and spirituals for union songs.

While the career of the Almanac Singers was brief, it exposed Hays to a wider audience. It enabled the singer-songwriter to perform as a solo artist and build a strong following. Hays performed with Guthrie, Houston, Fred Hellerman, Ronnie Gilbert, Pete Seeger and others, often for some union cause or in support of some downtrodden group.

In 1948, Hays formed the Weavers with Seeger, Ronnie Gilbert and Fred Hellerman. Hays, now a mature songwriter, wrote and co-wrote some of their best known songs, including "Kisses Sweeter Than Wine," and "If I Had a Hammer." The Weavers were a powerful voice before the folk boom and one of its main instigators.

In some ways, the Weavers became too powerful and vocal in their protests, because they ignited animosity. In the 1950s, hatred against the group reached a fever pitch as its members were heavily targeted during the communist hunts of the McCarthy era. Hays was attending a Paul Robeson performance in the fall of 1949 when the Peekskill Riots broke out among anti-communists. Hays, Guthrie and Seeger escaped possible death when the angry crowd entered the theater, threatening the audience and performers.

In 1950, Hays was blacklisted along with the rest of the group for communist activities. He was brought before the House Committee on Un-American Activities where he refused to testify. In 1952, the Weavers broke up because of their inability to perform on television or radio and in any music halls. Despite the breakup, their material made a big impact on the folk world and would continue to do so for a long time.

In 1955, the group's members reunited for a Carnegie Hall concert. It was an influential performance because it sparked the formation of future folk groups including the Limelighters, Peter, Paul and Mary, and the Kingston Trio, among others. The Weavers cut a number of albums including *Wasn't That a Time, Union Songs, Talking Union, Sod Buster Ballads, Deep Sea Chanteys, Gospel, Best of the Weavers, Goodnight Irene, Kisses Sweeter Than Wine*, and *Together Again*. Hays would continue appearing with the group, but also moonlighted with other groups, as well as enjoying a parallel solo career.

In 1958, he started a new project with a group called the Baby Sitters, which included Alan Arkin. They recorded children's albums and slowly Hays rebuilt his career. The rebound included concert appearances as well as sporadic reunions with the Weavers. Like so many others, Hays took some time to recover from the blacklisting.

In 1964, in deteriorating health, Hays played what seemed to be his last concert with the Weavers in Chicago. In 1967, he retreated to a reclusive place in New York where he tended to his organic vegetable garden, wrote and cooked. He enjoyed a circle of close friends who took care of him after he had both of his legs amputated. Hays, who suffered from diabetes, had become an alcoholic, which further fueled his downward trend. In 1969, he appeared with Arlo Guthrie in the film *Alice's Restaurant*, where he played a preacher.

In the 1970s, Hays took part in several Weavers reunions. By this point, his career had almost completely ceased because of poor health. Because the group's music was repackaged, he continued to earn modest royalties, but more importantly, was not totally forgotten. Aspiring folk artists learned how to play all of the group's songs from their records.

In June 1981, ill and wheelchair-bound, Hays pushed for one more get-together, which proved to be his last public performance. He died on August 26, 1981, from diabetic cardiovascular disease, before the release of the documentary film, *The Weavers: Wasn't That a Time!*

Lee Hays was a folk music stalwart. Once he had decided upon a musical career, he showed determination in his playing, writing and performing. Despite many obstacles, he succeeded in raising awareness of the social injustices of racism, inequality and violence.

Perhaps the best place to measure Hays's efforts is in his songs. Hays became an excellent songwriter, and the material which flowed from his imaginative pen reflected exactly what he was trying to achieve as an artist. The sophistication of his creativity explains why, 50 years after they were first recorded, many of the songs sound fresh today.

He wrote, collaborated on or revised a number of classics. A partial list includes "If I Had a Hammer," "Roll the Union On," "Raggedy, Raggedy, Are We," "The Rankin Tree," "On Top of Old Smoky," "Kisses Sweeter Than Wine," "Which Side Are You On?," "Plow the Fourth Bay Under," "Get Thee Behind Me, Satan" and "Goodnight Irene."

"If I Had a Hammer," written in collaboration with Pete Seeger, is a classic anthem of the goal the two had of creating a just society for all races, genders and creeds. "Roll the Union On" supported workers in their search for better wages and fairer treatment. "Which Side Are You On?" was a straightforward song about choosing between the establishment and those interested in making changes. In the 1960s, it would become a mini-anthem about the Vietnam War during the folk boom.

Hays had a resounding vocal delivery and sang bass with the Weavers.

Although his solo material was strong, in an ensemble situation, his deep, rich voice was much more pronounced. Hays contributed greatly to the lasting quality of the classic material.

Hays was instrumental in laying down the framework as a member of the Almanac Singers and, more importantly, the Weavers. Their songs were political, but also had a certain commercial element which influenced a great number of aspiring singers. In the 1960s, many borrowed from the group's catalog, including the Limelighters, Peter, Paul and Mary, the Byrds, the Kingston Trio, Joan Baez, Bob Dylan, the Rooftop Singers, Frank Hamilton, and the Tarriers, among others.

Despite being blacklisted by the government, Hays and the Weavers continued to struggle and make music. This rebellious attitude lent potency to the singer songwriters of folk's heyday. This was why they had such a huge influence on the Weavers' musical descendants.

The 1940s were truly Hays's greatest decade. Alone and as a member of the Almanac Singers and the Weavers, he laid down the foundation for the folk boom through recordings, political activism and concerts. The songs Hays recorded in this era became part of the repertoires of dozens of artists who starred in the folk revival.

Lee Hays was a man of principle whose beliefs could not be shaken. He yearned for a better world, one with less violence, racism and injustice. Through his political music he managed to make the world a better place for the working class, the poor and the downtrodden. The lonesome traveler's journey was one that inspired countless others and continues to do so.

DISCOGRAPHY:

The Secret Life, Lee Hays.

Josh White (1914–1969)
Folk-Blues Protest

Although folk was the main musical style utilized to bring about social change, other genres contributed. The blues, the outspoken musical language of poor African Americans, often illustrated their frustrating plight. Sometimes the two genres would be combined, creating a special force. One of the best practitioners was Josh White.

White was born February 11, 1914, in Greenville, South Carolina, the son of a minister who was a strict disciplinarian. The elder White hoped that his son would someday become a soldier in the fight against unfair state and local laws designed to circumvent the federal government's attempt to bring about justice for everyone. Instead, White would use music as a weapon of change.

White began his musical career in the church choir, and from an early age understood the power of song. At seven, a racial incident left him fatherless, and family responsibilities fell squarely on his shoulders. In order to support his mother and siblings, he accepted a job with a street singer named Blind Man Arnold.

The veteran street performer realized that the young boy had marketable talent and utilized the potential to his advantage. Although White never received much formal education, the lessons he learned from Arnold, as well as others, including Blind Lemon Jefferson, Blind Blake and Blind Joe Taggart, would prove to be invaluable.

White took up the guitar and adopted the styles of master players like Jefferson, Blake, and others. In 1932, he cut his first blues records and in a later session recorded some gospel material. During this period some of his more famous songs included "Jesus Gonna Make Up My Dying Bed," "Blood Red River," "Low Cotton," "Lay Some Flowers on My Grave," "Lord I Want to Die Easy" (covered by many artists), "Paul and Silas Bound in Jail," "Black Man," "Silicosis Is Killing Me," and "When the Sun Goes Down."

He formed a group called Josh White and the Carolinians, which included his brother Billy, Carrington Lewis, Sam Gary and Bayard Rustin. In 1963, the latter, a civil rights activist, would be instrumental in the March on Washington. The group performed in Harlem and one night the producers of the Broadway musical *John Henry* spotted White, who seemed to be the answer to their prayers. Although the play didn't have a long run on Broadway, it introduced him to the political set, including Woody Guthrie, Burl Ives and the Golden Gate Quartet.

White formed a duo with Huddie Ledbetter and they enjoyed a six-month residency at the Village's Vanguard nightclub, which became legendary. That would lead to other opportunities to record as well as to appear in film shorts. White — known as a blues and folksinger — began to incorporate more political elements in his music because of the Leadbelly influence.

Some time later, White teamed with Libby Holman — a white woman — causing a major sensation as the first ever inter-racial male and female act to appear in segregated venues. They recorded and performed together for six years. Although they broke new ground, they paid a heavy toll for such a bold endeavor, facing heavy racial tensions at many venues.

White recorded with Sidney Bechet as well as the Carolinians, including the controversial album, *Chain Gang*. He also continued to build a parallel solo career. At this point, the folk-blues singer was one of the most prominent artists in the public eye.

In 1940, near the Christmas holidays, White and the rest of the Golden Gate Quartet performed at a Library of Congress concert. A month later, they played at President Roosevelt's inauguration. Despite the segregation which still existed throughout much of the country, White was able to overcome racial barriers.

He reinvented himself as a mature performer whose outspoken viewpoints and sophistication won him audiences both white and African American. He recorded "One Meatball," an adaptation of an old English folk standard, that become a million seller. A diverse array of artists from the Andrews Sisters to Bing Crosby, and Dave Van Ronk, Ry Cooder, Lightnin' Hopkins and Lonnie Donegan recorded the tune.

Other material from this era included "Jelly, Jelly," "The House I Live In (What Is America to Me)," and "Waltzing Matilda," a song Frank Sinatra would take high into the charts. White rewrote many other songs such as "St. James Infirmary," "Lass with the Delicate Air," "John Henry," "Joshua Fit the Battle of Jericho," "The Riddle Song (I Gave My Love a Cherry)," "Evil Hearted Man," "Miss Otis Regrets," "The House of the Rising Sun," and "Strange Fruit."

By 1945, he was one of the most popular singers of the era, and a true multi-media star. He continued to perform at the Café Society nightclub, hosted a national radio show, and appeared in radio dramas based on the plays of Norman Corwin, as well as in musicals, and Hollywood movies including *The Crimson Canary, Dreams That Money Can Buy,* and *The Walking Hills.* He also managed to use his fame to promote unknown singers such as Jamaican Josephine Premice, and later Pearl Primus.

On the folk-protest front, he was a leading proponent of the civil rights movement that originated in the 1940s. The struggle for equality was a theme that ran through White's musical repertoire and vibrated with a particular vitality. He was a much sought-after spokesman at human rights rallies and his politically charged material would gather attention from the wrong people during the McCarthy era.

In the 1940s, the Café Society nightclub in New York served as a base of operations for White. The venue was one of the few places where caucasians and blacks could sit together as equals. The interracial mix fueled his songwriting during the era when he shared the stage with Fletcher Henderson's Orchestra, Billie Holiday, Atlanta blues figure Buddy Moss, jazz pianist Mary Lou Williams, and political folkies Guthrie, Pete Seeger, Burl Ives and Lee Hays.

Throughout the 1940s, White was closely associated with the Roosevelts. Because of this important political association he was able to record inflammatory material without repercussions. His album *Southern Exposure* included the title song "Uncle Sam Says," "Jim Crow Train," "Bad Housing Blues,"

"Defense Factory Blues," and "Hard Time Blues." He gave several White House command performances during President Roosevelt's long tenure. Later, White teamed up with Eleanor Roosevelt on her speaking engagements as the United Nations ambassador for war relief. The two toured overseas, and while she addressed large, enthusiastic crowds, he played guitar and sang.

In the 1950s, that close political association would end when he was labeled a communist sympathizer, which threatened to destroy his career. The Café Society was cited as one of the major "red" hot spots in the country, and since it was White's home base, there was no way he could escape from the backlash.

He volunteered to report to the HUAC and his testimony was turned against him. For example, he was accused of providing a list of people who were suspected communists, which was later proven false, but the damage could not be undone. Much of his fan base would be angered at comments which were wrongly interpreted, and he would have no choice but to relocate to England.

From 1950 to 1955, he hosted his own BBC radio show, and recorded more songs, including "On Top of Old Smoky," "Lonesome Road," "I Want You and Need You," "Wandering," "Molly Malone" and "I'm Going to Move to the Outskirts of Town." He also toured throughout Europe and revived his sagging career. In a short five years, White made a vital impact on the folk music scene.

He returned home and recorded his 25th anniversary album on the Elektra label. In 1963, President John F. Kennedy invited him to be part of the television special *Dinner with the President.* White resumed his political views and was present at the historic March on Washington. He eventually won back some of his lost fan base, but never returned to the level of popularity he had enjoyed earlier in his career.

In 1965, he performed at the inauguration of President Lyndon Johnson. White returned to television and made several appearances on *The Merv Griffin Show, Hugh Hefner's Playboy's Penthouse* and *Hootenanny,* as well as on various Canadian programs. The folksinger would also star in two music specials aired in Sweden, proving that he still retained some global appeal.

As far back as 1961, he had begun to suffer health problems, and survived three major heart attacks, as well as numerous other ailments. However, on September 6, 1969, he died on the operating table. He was 55 years old.

Josh White was a folk-blues spark plug. He cleverly managed to mesh the two styles into one cohesive sound which enabled him to create many potent songs. His songs were catchy, appealing to a broad listening public. His political views separated him from the rest of the folk-blues practitioners.

There was an intriguing catch to White's total delivery. He had a deep, melodious voice which allowed him to sing both folk and blues with equal power. His vocal skills also enabled the gifted artist to belt out protest ballads with a particular conviction. This wide range appealed to all listeners, both white and African American.

He was an interesting guitarist who was able to blend his good voice with solid instrumental abilities. His Piedmont-based style was a combination of intricate fingerpicking and folk strumming. Other musicians sought to imitate his guitar style. He did not use complicated chord patterns, but was an adequate player.

He was also a sexy entertainer. During concerts, he unbuttoned his shirt, baring his chest in a style many, including Harry Belafonte, Robert Plant of Led Zeppelin fame, and dozens of heavy metal stars, would copy. The sensually charged performances gained him many female admirers.

Because of his very distinct style, White influenced a number of artists. A partial list includes Blind Boy Fuller, Brownie McGhee, Pete Seeger, Lena Horne, Nat King Cole, Harry Belafonte, Lonnie Donegan, Eartha Kitt, Alexis Korner, Odetta, Ray Charles, Elvis Presley, the Kingston Trio, the Clancy Brothers, Tommy Makem, Merle Travis, Dave Van Ronk, Peter, Paul and Mary, Bob Dylan, Eric Weissberg, Judy Collins, Mike Bloomfield, Danny Kalb, Roger McGuinn, David Crosby, Richie Havens, Don McLean, Roy Harper, Ry Cooder, John Fogerty, Eva Cassidy, Pearl Primus, Josephine Premice, Josh White, Jr., Jackie Washington and the Chambers Brothers.

Josh White, Jr., would follow in the footsteps of his famous father, drawing musical inspiration from him. The young man would become a singer-songwriter, guitarist, actor, educator and social activist. In 1987, Josh Jr. would release the Grammy nominated *Jazz, Ballads* and *Blues*, which celebrated his father's music. In 1996, his second tribute effort, *House of the Rising Son*, appeared. Two of the elder White's daughters, Carolyn Fern and Judy, performed and recorded with their dad.

White gave the world a number of unforgettable songs. A partial list includes "One Meatball," "Uncle Sam Says," "Jim Crow Train," "Bad Housing Blues," "Defense Factory Blues," "Southern Exposure," "Hard Time Blues," "Beloved Comrade," "Freedom Road," "Free and Equal Blues," "House I Live In (What Is America to Me)," "Help the Blind," "On Top of Old Smoky," "Lonesome Road," "I Want You and Need You," "Wandering," "Molly Malone," and "I'm Going to Move to the Outskirts of Town."

He was greatly admired throughout the musical community. He was praised by Elvis Presley, Lonnie Donegan, John Fogerty, Bill Wyman, Jimmy Page, George Harrison, Charlie Watts, David Crosby, the Chambers Brothers, Janis Joplin, Scotty Moore, Phish, Ry Cooder, John Renbourn, John

Fahey, Robert Hunter, Eddie Cochrane, Gene Vincent, Don McLean, Richie Havens, Judy Collins, Bob Dylan, Bob Shane, Mary Travers, Lee Hayes, Pete Seeger, Oscar Brand, Liam Clancy, Merle Travis, and Eric Weissberg. Others, like producer Mickey Most, writer Langston Hughes and record company owner Jac Holzman, also spoke highly of him.

White appeared in a number of films including *The Crimson Canary, Dreams That Money Can Buy,* and *The Walking Hills,* as well as the posthumous productions *The Guitar of Josh White* and *Josh White: Free and Equal Blues/Rare Performances.* In addition, his songs would appear in the films *Earl Robinson: Ballad of an American, Jazz, Episode Seven: "Dedicated to Chaos," Strange Fruit, Red Tailed Angels: The Story of the Tuskegee Airmen,* and *Negroes with Guns.*

He was not the sole practitioner of the folk-blues style. Others included Brownie McGhee, Sam "Lightnin'" Hopkins, Huddie "Leadbelly" Ledbetter, Skip James, Sonny Terry, Richie Havens, Mississippi John Hurt, and Mississippi Fred McDowell. Like them, the folk boom revived his career.

In the 1940s, White was an important performer who helped pave the way for the folk boom that would occur a decade later. He broke barriers and ignited his performances with politically charged songs. His music had an international appeal that has survived the test of time. It is still performed to this day.

A number of songs paid tribute to White. Bob Gibson and Shel Silverstein wrote and recorded "Heavenly Choir," which also honored Hank Williams, Sr., and Janis Joplin. Peter Yarrow of Peter, Paul, and Mary fame penned "Goodbye Josh" on his first solo album. Jack Williams included "A Natural Man" on his *Walkin' Dreams* CD. In 1998, White appeared on a postage stamp. A long-running stage play entitled *JOSH: The Man & His Music* starred his son.

Josh White was an important figure in American musical history for decades. He was instrumental in the development of the hybrid style as an important social tool and his legacy lives on through his children and countless other performers. He made a lasting impact with his folk-blues protest.

DISCOGRAPHY:

Josh White Sings, Vol. 1, Mercury MG-25015.
Ballads, Vol. 2, Decca D-5247.
Strange Fruit, Emarcy MG-26010.
The Story of John Henry, Elektra 701.
Josh White Program, London 341.
Josh White's Blues, Mercury MG-20203.
Stories, Vol. 2, Paramount 166.
Chain Gang Songs, Elektra EK-158.
Ballads & Blues, Elektra EK-114.

The Beginning, Mercury 20724.
Josh White, Decca D 8665.
Roots of the Blues, Legacy 406.
Blues and..., Wooded Hill 16.
Empty Bed Blues, Sepia Tone/Stone 14.
Ballads, Decca 0–5082.
Josh at Midnight, Elektra 14.
Josh White Sings, Vol. 2 (Blues), Stinson 338.
Josh White, London EM-102.
25th Anniversary Album, Elektra EK-123.
Josh White 1933–1944, Best of Blues 7.
Complete Recorded Works, Vol. 1 (1929–1933), Document 5194.
Complete Recorded Works, Vol. 2 (1933–1935), Document 5195.
Complete Recorded Works, Vol. 3 (1935–1940), Document 5196.
Complete Recorded Works, Vol. 4 (1940–41), Document 5405.
Sings the Blues, Collectables 5602.
Blues Singer 1932–1936, Columbia/Legacy 67001.
The Legendary Josh White, Collector's Edition 4.
Complete Recorded Works, Vol. 5 (1944), Document 5571.
Complete Recorded Works, Vol. 6 (1944–1945), Document 5572.
Free & Equal Blues, Smithsonian Folkways 40081.
Southern Exposure, Pearl 7810.
The Best of Josh White, Tradition 1082.
Remaining Titles: 1941–1947, Document 1013.
Hard Time Blues, Columbia River 120010.
The Legendary, Magnum Collectors 3.
The Essential, Classic Blues 20005.
Blues: 1932–1945 [live], Frémeaux & Associés 264.
From New York to London, Jasmine 3004.
Josh at Midnight/Ballads and Blues, Collectables 7463.
Blues and Ballads, Acrobat 166.
The Elektra Years, Rhino Handmade 7879.
Wanderings, ASV/Living Era 5551.
Comes A-Visitin, Comes A-Singin', Empire Musicwerks 450853.
Blood Red River, Blue Orchid 201.
Presenting Josh White, Signature 2175.
Bluesman, Guitar Evangelist, Folksinger, Saga Blues 5302038.
Roots N Blues: Blues Singer, 1932–1936, Blue Label 42452.
Josh White, Folk Music 209.
The Best of Josh White, Elektra 75008.

Cisco Houston (1918–1961)

The Pure Voice

Like other styles, folk music boasts an interesting array of individual talent which helped shape the music. Among the most distinguishing features are vocal tone, texture and ability. While some traditional singers sound rough, others have a smooth delivery. One such individual was a man whose voice was instantly recognizable, Cisco Houston.

Gilbert Vandine Houston was born on August 18, 1918, in Wilmington, Delaware. He derived his musical background from his North Carolina father and his Appalachian mother and grandmother who were from Virginia. Before his teens the family relocated to southern California, which provided him with another source of music: cowboy, railroad worker and hobo tunes.

Although he suffered physical challenges, he indulged in theater and art as an elementary student, performing in a variety of plays. While in college, he continued to hone his acting skills and was involved in local thespian groups. He seemed destined to be a Hollywood star.

Along the way, Houston learned to play the guitar and honed his abilities until he was proficient enough to play in front of an audience. He was also collecting folksongs, which were added to an ever-growing repertoire, many derived from family sources. Since cowboy songs were his favorite, he found work on Western radio stations and in various clubs that catered to that style of music.

In the early years of the Great Depression, his father left the family, and a young, disillusioned Houston decided to see America. He departed with a brother and the two trekked throughout the United States. It was the first of many such personal voyages for Houston. Along the way he picked up the stage name "Cisco." His wanderlust eventually took him full circle and he returned to California.

Although Houston continued to perform in various theater groups, by this point in time he had no real aspiration to pursue an acting career. Instead, he wanted to become a folksinger. However, while performing in a play, Houston befriended actor Will Geer. One day, they heard Woody Guthrie on a local radio station and decided to go down to meet the famous entertainer.

It wasn't long before Guthrie and Houston formed a solid friendship that would last for the rest of their respective lives. They performed on Guthrie's radio show. Houston, who had a smooth voice, was a perfect counterpoint to his partner's rougher-edged sound. The harmonies between the two created magic which would become legendary.

The pair performed at migrant camps, eventually with Burl Ives and Geer. When Guthrie decided to relocate to New York, Houston accompanied him, but they found little work. Houston returned to California and took whatever work he could find, including a stint as a street barker.

Eventually, Houston and Guthrie reunited and traveled throughout America again. At the migrant camps, they sang songs that promoted union and workers' rights. The political emphasis in their work was new for Houston but he adapted to it very quickly. Houston quickly became a champion of the downtrodden. He understood fully the suffering of the unemployed, who came from all corners of the United States.

In 1940, Houston joined the Merchant Marines and performed with Guthrie as a duo, and as part of the Almanac Singers whenever his schedule allowed. Eventually Guthrie also joined the war effort and the two survived torpedo attacks on various dangerous missions. They honed their singing skills and wrote new material while completing each tour of duty.

After he was discharged, Houston, who had never lost his wanderlust, traveled throughout the country. He occasionally returned to New York and during those brief stints, he stayed with Leadbelly and his wife. Houston continued to write songs and performed at every opportunity, but also supplemented his income with odd jobs as a laborer, cowboy, and part-time actor. The varied skills enabled him to keep body and soul together.

When his good friend Guthrie started to record for the Folkways label, Houston sang background. Not long after, Houston made his own recordings for the company, which opened many doors. It was evident that he was more than Guthrie's shadow and had a solid amount of talent.

In 1948, Houston put his acting talents to good use, appearing in the Broadway musical, *The Cradle Will Rock*. Houston spent time in Hollywood as well, where he found lucrative work, appearing in a number of films. But the road called again and soon he was traveling with Guthrie, criss-crossing the country singing folksongs, often to help out the less fortunate.

Throughout the 1950s, Houston was very active and split his time between recording for the Decca label and appearing on television programs, including his own *The Gil Houston Show*, broadcast on the International Network. By 1955, he was seen on more than 500 stations and rode the charts with the original hit "Crazy Heart." Later, Jackie Paris would record a version and enjoy moderate success, which helped establish Houston as a songwriter.

Like so many other folk performers, he suffered a decline in popularity during the McCarthy era and eventually his TV show was cancelled. Houston returned to the Golden State where he earned a marginal living as a folksinger. He also continued to travel from one end of the country to the other to play music in support of social justice and equality for all.

Despite blacklisting, Houston was able to record sporadically for a number of labels, including Folkways, Decca and Vanguard, as well as smaller, independent studios. He guest-starred on a number of radio shows and pleased listeners with his smooth voice. Despite being called a communist, Houston never compromised his left-wing political views.

Houston returned to regular work once the McCarthy era was over. In 1959, he toured India for 12 weeks, on a tour organized by the Indo-American Society and United States Information Service to broaden the relationship between the two countries. Back in the United States, Houston returned to television, where he performed as narrator and singer on the show *Folk Sound, U.S.A.* It was the dawn of the folk revival and the next few years would be the golden era.

Houston continued to build momentum. He recorded for the Vanguard label and also played at the vaunted Newport Folk Festival. After years of struggling to establish a career as an entertainer and surviving the blacklisting of the McCarthy era, he was poised to reap the benefits. However, on April 21, 1961, cancer robbed the folk establishment of one of its most important performers.

Cisco Houston had a magical voice, an easy guitar style, concern for the downtrodden, a lust for traveling, defiance in defending his beliefs in the face of government scrutiny, and a flair for the dramatic. He is forever linked with Woody Guthrie, was a member of the groundbreaking Almanac Singers, and enjoyed a solid career as an individual performer. He was known for his ability to travel despite very poor eyesight.

It was often said that Houston didn't have a true folk voice, because his was too polished. Arguably, his vocal timber was much smoother than Guthrie's or almost any of the other folksingers on the circuit at the time. There was no pain or roughness in his delivery with which the downtrodden — miners, union activists, railroad workers, hobos — could identify, but ironically these were the people he sang about and fought for his entire career.

Although he began his recording work by providing background harmony vocals for Guthrie, eventually Houston cut his own songs. His excellent vocal quality shined forth on the solo records. His delivery was so powerful that he could excel as part of a group situation or as a solo entertainer.

Houston recorded songs from a variety of sources including Woody Guthrie, Leadbelly, Alan Lomax, Merle Travis, Joe Hill, Dorsey M. Dixon, Jimmie Davis, and Wade Mainer, among others. Like other folksingers, he sang traditional tunes, but with that unmistakable voice, Houston put an undeniable stamp on each number. He also recorded original material.

He recorded a good number of songs as a solo artist. A partial list includes "This Train," "Roll On, Columbia," "Dark as a Dungeon," "Old Blue," "Badman Ballad," "Diamond Joe," "Big Rock Candy Mountain," "So Long It's

Been Good to Know Yuh," "Hard Travelin'," "Pretty Boy Floyd," "Talking Dust Bowl Blues," "I Ain't Got No Home," "Hobo Bill," "The Strawberry Roan," "The Intoxicated Rat," "Ship in the Sky," "What Did the Deep Sea Say," "Mysteries of a Hobo's Life," "900 Miles," "Great July Jones," "The Sister's Lament," "Columbus Stockade," and "Skip to My Lou." No matter the source, he made every number fun.

He had a significant influence on a number of artists including Utah Phillips, Phil Ochs, Tom Paxton, Oscar Brand, Pete Seeger, Burl Ives, Sonny Terry, Brownie McGhee, Leadbelly, Ramblin' Jack Elliott, Peter La Farge, and Jackie Greene. He also had a profound effect on his traveling partner, Woody Guthrie, who was more famous than Houston, but relied on his friend for advice and as a comrade dedicated to the cause.

Houston, Guthrie and Leadbelly were responsible for bringing folk into the modern, post-war era. He helped lay the groundwork for the boom years of the late 1950s and 1960s. Sadly, just as his career seemed to be on the verge of exploding, Houston was diagnosed with terminal cancer and didn't live to enjoy the benefits of what he had helped create.

Cisco Houston was a folk music rock. The talented entertainer left a solid body of work in the music and acting fields.

DISCOGRAPHY:

900 Miles and Other Railroad Ballads, Smithsonian Folkways Fe-2013.
Cowboy Ballads, Smithsonian Folkways FA-2022.
Folk Songs, Smithsonian Folkways Fe-2346.
Hard Travelin', Smithsonian Folkways Fe-2042.
Cisco Houston Sings the Songs of Woody Guthrie, Vanguard 2131.
I Ain't Got No Home, Vanguard 73006.
Sings Songs of the Open Road, Smithsonian Folkways 2480.
Cisco Houston & Woody Guthrie, Ember 135.
Traditional Songs of the Old West, Stinson 37.
Nursery Rhymes, Games & Folk Songs, Smithsonian Folkways 7606.
The Folkways Years, 1944–1961, Smithsonian Folkways 40059.
Legendary, Collector's Edition 13.
Best of the Vanguard Years, Vanguard 79574.

Joe Glazer (1918–2006)

Labor's Troubadour

When musicians began to use folk as a powerful tool of change, awareness, protest, and political clout, the genre took on a new dimension. Suddenly, traditional tunes were more than mere novelty numbers and became anthems for unions across the land. One of the best artists at welding lyrics with inspirational music was labor's troubadour, Joe Glazer.

Glazer was born in 1918 in New York City. He began his musical career in synagogues, but the singing cowboys of the Hollywood set — Gene Autry and Roy Rogers — gave him his early inspiration. He bought a guitar from the Sears catalog and took lessons via the WPA program. Although his father was a proud member of a union, young Glazer would not join his songs with his political beliefs until much later.

In 1936, he arrived at Brooklyn College and began to develop his political worldview. But he stayed away from the campus radicals. The young songwriter wanted to become a working tunesmith and poured his efforts into this pursuit. He tasted brief success when his novelty ditty "Yogi, Yogi, the Fakir Man," became a minor hit for Reggie Childs.

He served with the Theatre Arts Committee, which was aligned with the Cabaret T.A.C., and just before the end of World War II, he became the assistant education director for the New York City Textile Workers Union. Suddenly, after years of being surrounded by political groups, he found himself in the line of fire.

He turned his songwriting skills to labor pieces and lore. Glazer's job included travel. During a tour of Southern textile communities he heard the work hymns which truly sparked his imagination. A short time later he recorded his first album, *Eight New Songs for Labor*, issued on a private label under the imprint of the Congress of Industrial Organizations.

Although it wasn't commercially appealing, it made an impact on the protest circuit. Many different artists learned the songs on the album because of their power and beauty. Glazer eventually became a known commodity around union folk circles for his songwriting abilities. While others like Woody Guthrie, Fred Hellerman, Cisco Houston, Pete Seeger, Lee Hays, and Ronnie Gilbert were making history, labor's troubadour was carving out his own niche.

In 1950, he relocated to Akron, Ohio, home of the tire industry. He was named education director of the United Rubber Workers-CIO, an important position that allowed him to be directly involved in the union struggles. He was passionate in his pursuit of better conditions for the working man because he truly believed in the cause. About this time he befriended Bill Friedland.

Friedland was born on Staten Island, the son of Russian immigrants who were associated with the Workmen's Circle. As a student he was drawn to Trotskyism and later moved on to a splinter group who called themselves the Shackmanites. This organization wanted to colonize the labor communities of America. As a result, Friedland ended up in Detroit as an assistant to Bill Kemsley, education director of the Michigan State CIO.

Friedland, a self-taught singer and musician, had collected hundreds of labor songs through the years, many with an anti–Communist slant. In 1952, Glazer and Friedland united their talents to record the album *Ballads for Sectarians*, released on Kemsley's Labor Arts label. Although the geographical distance between the two made it impossible to rehearse on a regular basis, they did collaborate on a second union album, *Songs of the Wobblies*.

They made a good duo, but Friedland tired of the labor movement and enrolled in college, completed his doctorate and left the world of protest songs behind. Glazer continued union activity and recorded a solo album on the Labor Arts label. In the 1960 presidential race, he threw his support and talent behind Hubert Humphrey's failed bid.

Glazer continued to broadcast his labor beliefs in different forms, including in a collaboration with Canadian folklorist Edith Fowke on the book *Songs of Work and Freedom*. In 1961, he further broadened his reach when he accepted a position with the U.S. Information Agency. He jumped at the opportunity to instill the message of the American labor movement overseas.

During his time abroad, he preached respect for the average world laborer. He did it through song and left a definite impact on everyone who heard him. Glazer proved that the struggle of the working person was international, not regional.

In 1968, after years of recording on fledgling labels, Glazer formed his own company, Collector, and released several albums, including *Joe Glazer Sings Labor Songs, Glazer Sings Glazer, American Dream,* and the 12" single "The Ballad of Bobby Fischer." This was one of the most prolific periods of his entire career, which further cemented him as a champion in union circles. Later he would record a new generation of singers/labor activists on his label.

By 1979, he was a veteran of organizing groups, promoting unions and pushing work songs. That year, he brought 14 musicians to Silver Spring, Maryland. More than a dozen artists attended the event, which became a yearly occurrence called the Great Labor Arts Exchange. In 1984, the Labor Heritage Foundation was formed. It was dedicated to the preservation of the musical history of the workers' movement.

In 1997, Glazer received the Joe Hill Award in honor of his dedication to union struggles. He also published his autobiography, *Labor's Troubadour*. In 2005, he donated the entire holdings of Collector Records to the Smithsonian Center for Folklife and to Cultural Heritage's Ralph Rinzler Folklife Archives. He was beginning to slow down because of his age.

While he enjoyed retirement, he was often remembered for his work in the struggle for workers' rights. On September 19, 2006, Glazer died at his home in Silver Springs, of non–Hodgkin's lymphoma. He was 88 years old.

Joe Glazer was a labor activist with musical talent. While others used their skills and abilities to organize rallies, marches and protests, he inspired striking union brothers and sisters. Although his catalog was not as extensive as those of other folk artists, it included a number of tunes popular throughout the nation and the world.

Glazer was a pivotal player in the political connection between folk and unions. Along with Woody Guthrie, Cisco Houston, Lee Hays, Fred Hellerman, Ronnie Gilbert, and Josh White, he devoted his musical skills to the betterment of the common worker. His contributions were so integral to the cause that that he was dubbed labor's troubadour.

Like all of those mentioned above, Glazer drew much inspiration from Joe Hill, the notorious labor activist and agitator. Although not as infamous as Hill, Glazer was able to establish his own place within the folk movement.

Although he recorded more than 30 albums, very few were commercial successes and most appeared on obscure labels that have since been discontinued. Sadly, Glazer's catalog reflects this. Very few recordings are available to the public. A partial list of his efforts includes *Eight New Songs for Labor, Ballads for Sectarians, Songs of the Wobblies, Songs of Work and Freedom, Joe Glazer Sings Labor Songs, Glazer Sings Glazer,* and *American Dream.*

Glazer's lack of commercial appeal doesn't diminish his contributions. However, because he never made commercially promoted records, his name does not loom as large as those of Woody Guthrie, Pete Seeger, Cisco Houston, Lee Hays, Ronnie Gilbert, Fred Hellerman, and others. Glazer was not connected to any of them and represents an entire new dimension in social activism. His friends, part of the labor movement, included the Elm City Four. They cut a few of his songs as well as other material, including their own version of "We Shall Overcome." The group consisted of union members who teamed with the folksinger for a brief time. Although they had some talent, they would never be mistaken for members of the Almanac Singers or the Weavers.

Joe Glazer was a passionate activist and labor organizer. He lent his talents to the movement to better the condition of the common worker. Although he remains an obscure figure in some corners, his contributions to the political dimension of folk music is solid. He proved that he was labor's troubadour.

Discography:

Songs of Joe Hill, Smithsonian Folkways 2039.

Pete Seeger (1919–)

Twentieth Century Folk Man

The evolution of folk music in the past hundred years has taken the style from traditional music of the common man to an instrument of social change covering causes such as the environment, the plight of humanity and population growth. Many have utilized protest songs to bring about social change and fight injustice. While numerous artists have risen mixing music and politics, none has done more for the genre than Pete Seeger.

Seeger was born on May 3, 1919, in New York City. His father, Charles, was a musicologist and conductor and his mother, Constance, was a violinist and teacher. Both had served on the faculty of Juilliard and were also very much into political causes which they instilled into their young son. Initially, Seeger was not impressed with his parents' music and yearned for a career as a painter. However, he changed his mind when he took up the banjo.

His father married Ruth Crawford when Seeger was 10. Later the young Seeger attended Avon Old Farms and was selected for Camp Rising Sun, an international scholarship program. Seeger discovered the ukulele, but eventually would turn to the banjo as his primary instrument. He would later add the 12-string guitar.

He studied sociology at Harvard, building a platform which would serve him well later in life. But he never graduated. Instead, he hooked up with Alan Lomax and traveled the American South in search of authentic folk, blues and country tunes. During this period, he also began to write work songs, lullabies, traditional numbers and ballads, which formed the basis of his repertoire. The raw material he collected from his experiences formed the cycle of songs which would someday make him famous.

In 1940, at a migrant benefit concert, he befriended Woody Guthrie. The two shared many of the same beliefs and joined forces to form the Almanac Singers, the first musical group to sing political material. The group would boast links to other radicals including Lee Hays, Millard Lampell, Sis Cunningham, Sonny Terry, Brownie McGhee, Leadbelly, Josh White, Burl Ives and Richard Dyer-Bennet. Although the group's tenure was brief, its existence would influence folk groups for sixty years.

In 1942, Seeger was drafted into the army and spent his time in the South Pacific. After his release, he continued wandering, but also concentrated on a musical career and performed at various venues, including churches, parks and taverns. In 1943, he married Toshi-Aline Ohta and half a century later they were still together.

Later in the decade, Seeger, Hays, Ronnie Gilbert and Fred Hellerman